THE FAMILY

The image of the family has been further complicated by differences based on class, region, religion and ethnicity. We now recognize that ethnic minority communities have household patterns that are linked strongly to their heritage and may be different from the majority population. Sociologists have documented this diversity in family structure, roles and relationships, not only for Asian and African-Caribbean families, but also for Cypriot, Jewish, Irish, Italian and Polish communities. There is also regional variation in family structure within the UK and factors such as the total fertility rate (TFR – the number of children an average women would have assuming that she lives her full productive lifetime) can vary considerably.

Sociological perspectives

As social change has occurred in society, the sociological study of the family has been adapted and reshaped so that we no longer think of 'the family' but of 'families and households' – such has been the extent of change. As a reaction against the harmonious functionalist picture painted of the family, Marxist sociologists such as Zaretsky (1976) have been more critical of the family as an institution. Zaretsky argued that the family enables the continued existence of capitalism by rearing and socializing the new generation of workers, whilst providing a haven for current workers to escape from the daily toil. The family may provide a strong motivation to work and a sense of responsibility, which acts as a disincentive to be critical of the system (see Chapter 4).

Feminist sociologists such as Ann Oakley have also focused their attention on areas that male sociologists have ignored. Oakley (1974a) argued that there was a patriarchal overview in much of sociology and especially in the study of the family. This malestream view made assumptions that there was a 'natural' or 'normal' family structure with the male head of the household/breadwinner and the female housewife and mother, and malestream research into family was affected by this ideology. Oakley wanted to show what women's lives were really like in the research that she carried out over several decades. She has published research that has looked at the sociology of housework (1974), childbearing (1979), becoming a mother, a sociology of childbirth (1980), and the history of medical care of pregnant women (1984), as well as publishing material related to feminist research methods throughout the 1990s. In 2005, *The Ann Oakley Reader – Gender, Women and Social Science* was published, which contains much of the work she has completed over the course more than 30 years.

Interpretivist sociological perspectives have concentrated on small-scale interactions within the family; the negotiation of meanings between members and the way in which the family can be a source of conflict, oppression and unhappiness for its members. Some of the earliest sources for this approach were R.D. Laing (1976) and David Cooper (1972), both radical psychiatrists, who believed that the intense interplay of emotions and power relationships within the confines of the family could lead to mental illness, particularly schizophrenia, in the young.

Since the end of the 1970s, with the election of the Thatcher Conservative government, there has also been a social-political perspective on the family which, although mainly outside of sociology, has had an impact on our thinking and views – the New Right (see Chapter 3). These commentators have stressed the harmful nature of the changes that have taken place within the family and advocate a return to traditional family values, morality, structure and relationships. John Major's 'back to basics' campaign in the 1990s was supposed to stimulate a return to Victorian values of family and home with two parents and their children, but became rather 'unstuck' when several Conservative MPs and cabinet ministers were found to be having extra-marital relationships and illegitimate children. In the early days of the 2010 Conservative/Liberal Democratic coalition government in the UK, one minister resigned because, in order to keep his gay relationship private, he had misrepresented his relationship with his partner in claiming Parliamentary expenses, and another left his wife for his mistress. These events suggest that supporting and maintaining 'traditional values' in an age of change is not straightforward.

Most recently, postmodernists have presented a further critique of the conventional sociological view and approach to the study of the family. Their argument is that we have now moved into a post-industrial age when choice and diversity are the key facets of society and, therefore, the family. Hence, family pluralism is the new order, where we adopt our own lifestyles and construct relationships that suit our needs at any one time. This approach also stresses the loss of traditional sources of identity such as the family, seeing the fragmentation of cultural patterns within the institution of the family as typical of postmodern society. The notion of *the family* – that is, the existence of one type of family or household – is dead. All living arrangements are open to negotiation, fluidity and change (Cheal 1993).

Another perspective relates to the notion of 'display' as a means to analyze and understand contemporary family practices. Finch (2007) adopts the discussion of this from Morgan's work on family practices (1996) as a starting point to define 'display' as the family 'doing' things rather than 'being' a family (p. 66). Essentially, the emphasis is on how individuals understand, interpret and display their behaviour in family relationships. Finch (2007) argues that the meanings of actions is part of the social nature of family practices, and actions and meanings need to be conveyed and understood by relevant family members to affirm these relationships as part of 'my family'. Essentially, 'display' is the many regular, routine practices in a family, such as reading a child a bedtime story or regularly phoning a relative to keep in touch, which taken together constitute family life.

Changing family and household patterns

The number of households in the UK in 2006 was 24.2 million according to *Social Trends 37* (ONS 2007), an increase of 5.6 million since 1971. The main reason for this increase is the trend towards smaller households with single person households rising from 18 per cent in 1971 to 29 per cent in 2006, and households containing six or more people declining from 6 per cent in 1971 to 2 per cent in 2006. Households containing a couple with dependent children fell from 35 per cent in 1971 to 22 per cent in 2006. There are variations in patterns when different characteristics such as ethnicity are taken into account. For example, British Asian households, notably Pakistani and Bangladeshi, are the largest, with an average household size of 4.1 and 4.4 respectively, with the white British household size being about 2.5, roughly half the size. Black Caribbeans and Africans are more likely than any other ethnic group of being lone-parent households. As mentioned, the increase in different family 'constellations' (Folgerø 2008) – such as

A family but not a household	Both a family and household	A household but not a family

You will have become aware whilst completing this task that other issues are important. First, is a childless couple a family? Second, is a couple who has children but are not married seen as a family? Finally, are lone parents or a gay couple families? Clearly, the interpretation of these situations may vary over time and from one culture to another. Your answers to these questions and Exercise 2.3 will partly depend on how you view these issues in society today.

Now you are ready to interpret and evaluate a number of possible ways of defining the family.

Ⓘ Ⓐ Ⓐⓝ Ⓔ

Exercise 2.5

Consider each of the following definitions. How accurate are they? How comprehensive and how useful are they? Write down at least one strength and one weakness of each definition.

- The family is a social group characterized by common residence, economic cooperation and reproduction. It includes adults of both sexes, at least two of whom maintain a socially approved sexual relationship, and one or more children, own or adopted, of the sexually cohabiting couple (Murdock 1949).
- A group of persons directly linked by kin connections, adult members of which assume responsibility of caring for children (Giddens 1993).
- A network of related kin (Goldthorpe 1987).
- A family is a married couple who live together in the same house.
- All the people we are related to by blood or marriage, the family of origin is the family we are born into (Lawson and Garrod (2007).
- All the persons living together in a household.

Which of the situations in Exercise 2.4 are not covered by one or more of the above definitions?

THE IDEOLOGY OF THE FAMILY

We have seen that, at any time and in any place, what is viewed at the 'normal' family will vary. Nevertheless, each of us will probably have a reasonably clear idea of what we mean when we talk about this institution in our everyday lives. Our belief in what is, for us, a normal family is heavily influenced by ideology – the systematic set of beliefs that usually serves the interests of a particular social group in society (Lawson and Garrod 2009). In the UK, it is often assumed that the normal family is the nuclear family – mother, father and children living together, with the mother looking after the home and family, and the father going out to work. This image or ideology is sometimes referred to as the 'Oxo' or 'cornflake packet' family because it has been consistently used in adverts to sell these products and consists of a happy family seated around a table eating a meal together. Of course, one of things we know about ideologies is that they represent a particular or partial view generated by those who are creating the images, in this case advertisers whose job it is to sell products.

The role of ideology

Ideology can shape our view of the world even though, as mentioned, it may be a partial or selective view. A set or system of ideas explains the way society is structured and give legitimacy to social actions and elements of culture.

Both Marxist and feminist sociologists refer to 'dominant ideologies' to describe the way those in authority or more powerful positions in society can produce a set of ideas that are adopted by those in less powerful positions (e.g. women and the working class). Dominant ideologies present aspects of the social world as natural, inevitable or universal, implying that alternative ways of thinking or behaving are unnatural or unusual. Alternatives can then be criticized. In the case of the nuclear family, as we have seen, we are surrounded by images of the 'normal', 'natural' family and are encouraged to see this pattern of the family as the norm and to strive to achieve this version of family life and family relationships. Often, other types of families are openly discouraged and seen as undesirable.

However, research by Gatrell (2008) and others suggests that there has been a change in views related to child care. Gatrell's qualitative research on heterosexual dual-earner families suggests that it is becoming much more 'normal' for fathers to play a significant role in the upbringing of their children, often sharing responsibilities right from moment their children are born. These fathers felt their relationships with their children were rewarding and took their child care responsibilities seriously, especially when their partner was combining motherhood with paid work. Gatrell also found that fathers were involved in many of the routine aspects of child care – such as feeding, bathing, taking to nursery – and not just the 'fun' activities often associated with the care of children. However, Gatrell concluded that the resistance to the role of fathers in child care by some mothers might relate to the expectation that men also take a 50:50 share in the housework, too (see Chapter 7).

Pressure/protest groups such Fathers4Justice and charities such as Families Need Fathers have also emerged, which suggests that more men want greater involvement with their children after divorce or marital breakdown. They argue that the acceptance of mothers as 'lead parents' needs to be challenged, and that fathers should have an equal say in the care of and contact with their children. High-profile protests by such groups – whose members dressed as Batman and Superman to scale the walls of Buckingham Palace in the necessarily live together or nearby but make a point of seeing each other regularly and make an effort to keep in touch.

Each individual within either of these structures is likely to be part of both a *family of origin* and a *family of procreation*. The first of these is the family which you are born into and by which you are raised, the second is the new family that you create and in which your family grow up. *Lone parents* or *single-parent families* where there is one parent raising children have become common in Western societies, with notable variations between ethnic and social class groups, and in some countries. The rise has been swift in Australia and Eire, but less rapid in predominantly Catholic countries such as France (Allan and Crow, 2001). However, most single-parent families are headed by women who are divorced, or who have never married, or have cohabited. Black Caribbeans and black Africans are more likely than other ethnic groups in the UK to be lone-parent households. One in four children lives in a lone-parent family usually headed by a woman. Lone-parent families are partly a consequence of the rise in divorce rates, but also as a result of the choices of many women to have children outside of a marriage or living with a partner. It should therefore be acknowledged that there is diversity in lone parenthood as well as commonalities. Income, the age of children, and the emotional and social support offered by kin and friends all interact to produce different experiences for those living in lone-parent households.

Another form of family which is growing in number is the *reconstituted* or *reordered* or *blended family*. This family comprises a couple, at least one of whom has been married and divorced before, and children from both present and previous marriage(s) – in other words, this family has step-parents, stepchildren and sometimes stepsiblings (see Chapter 8) . Since 1981, one in 10 divorcing men and women had had a previous marriage that also ended in divorce. There has also been a rise in *singletons* – people living by themselves, usually pensioners but also including young people, those divorced or separated and, increasingly, older women. Another increase has taken place in *empty-nest families* – where children have grown up and left home. However, there is evidence that older children, particularly sons, return to the family home at a later age. *Same-sex families* have been increasingly recognized since the Civil Partnerships Act in 2004 gave gay couples the same rights in law as those entering a civil marriage, and this is especially important in relation to parental responsibility for children. Also, with the increase in IVF as a reproductive technology and homosexual nuclear families, the emphasis on the family involving blood ties can be seen as weakening. Do these changes undermine the family, or simply recognize diversity in modern society? Sociologists (Weston 1991, Roseneil 2000, Folgerø 2008) are beginning to research these areas and find out how we give meaning to them, and how actors understand them.

For Donzelot (1980), the diversity in what constitutes a family would be evidence that, at any time in history, it is not possible to identify a dominant family form. The idea that there is an 'agreed' form of the family results from moral or ideological dominance and bears little, if any, relationship to actual families that exist at that time. Donzelot follows the work of Foucault in arguing that sociologists should study and analyze the actual practices of families and 'deconstruct' common-sense dominant forms of the family.

Patterns of marriage

Patterns of marriage vary considerably throughout the world. In Western societies, the only legal form of marriage is *monogamy* – a form of marriage in which an individual has only one spouse at any one time. The term *serial monogamy* has been used to describe having a number of different partners, but only one at a time.

Polygamy is where a spouse can marry more than one partner at a time. There are two types of *polygamy*. *Polygyny*, which is more common, is when a man can marry more than one wife at a time and is notably associated with the Islamic religion. It is a Muslim tradition to provide equally for all wives. *Polygyny* is often practiced in tribal societies where men spend time away hunting or caring for the cattle. *Polyandry* is quite rare and the opposite of *polygyny* – *polyandry* is where women take more than one husband at a time. In Nepal and Tibet, a woman of the Nyimba people may marry all the brothers in a family – this is termed *fraternal polyandry* and is seen as the best economic contract in an impoverished society where making a living is far from easy.

When considering the choice of a partner in some societies, there is free choice. In Britain, we tend to marry those of similar status, education and socio-economic background despite the supposed free choice. Notions of romantic love and belief in fate seem to give way to practical matters in our choice of partner. In Asian and African culture, there are *arranged marriages* with varying degrees of strictness, whereby parents and matchmakers play a role in the choice of marriage partners. Overwhelmingly, families wish their children to marry someone with whom they are compatible and whom they can learn to love and live with happily. However, a small minority of families have been known to kill children, usually daughters, who enter into 'inappropriate' relationships of which the family strongly disapprove, feeling their family honour has been compromised. *Forced marriage* is now a crime in the UK and shows recognition of the growing need to ensure young people can enter into freely arranged marriages. There is a Forced Marriage Unit at the Home Office and schools have been issued with guidelines to help reduce the 1600 reports of young persons, usually girls, being forced into marriages by monitoring those who 'disappear' from school registers around the age of 16.

Arranged marriage was common in Europe before the industrial revolution, particularly based upon social and economic factors, especially amongst royalty and the aristocracy. In some parts of central Europe, the landlord had to approve the prospective partners before a marriage could take place. In places such as Sri Lanka, much emphasis is placed on the prospective couple sharing a compatible or auspicious horoscope when wedding plans are being made.

Ⓔ

Exercise 2.7

The aim of this exercise is to develop your awareness of the nature and logic of different marriage patterns. Use the table below to list the advantages and disadvantages of 'free choice' and 'arranged' marriages for the individuals concerned, the family and society. If there are students who you know from a number of different cultures and background or heritages, you may already be familiar with different practices – this can add a great deal to your discussion and understanding.

	For the individual	For the family	For society
Advantages of arranged marriage			
Disadvantages of arranged marriage			
Advantages of free choice marriage			
Disadvantages of free choice marriage			

Formal and informal rules

There can often be rules about whom we are allowed to marry. These rules may be formal or informal, but will usually oblige individuals to marry either within or outside a particular social group. *Exogamy* means that a person must marry someone outside a social group – such as a clan, family, village or tribe. In the UK, a limited form of exogamy is built into the law in that we are not legally allowed to marry blood relatives who are only two steps away from us – we cannot marry our parents, our children, siblings (brothers or sisters), grandparents, grandchildren, aunts, or uncles. The closest relative we can marry is a cousin. *Endogamy* is the opposite – individuals must marry within a social group – such as kin groups, religion, age, social class, or region. The rules for endogamy are generally more flexible than those of exogamy but they can be very rigid for certain groups – such as closed religious sects. Do these rules apply in modern Britain?

There a number of other terms with which you should be aware. The terms *patriarchal* and *matriarchal* describe the focus of authority in the family. A patriarchal family is one in which the power and authority are vested in the father; in a matriarchal family, the mother is the focus of power and authority. Similarly, *patrilineal* inheritance is passed down the male line and *matrilineal* inheritance is passed down the female line. Inheritance can include goods, wealth, property, name, status, and title and so on. *Matrilocal* residence describes when a couple live with or near to the wife's parents, *patrilocal* residence is the arrangement where the couple live with or near to the husband's parents. If a couple live independently, away from both families of origin, this is known as *neo-local* residence.

ALTERNATIVES TO THE FAMILY?

The Nayar of Kerala in Southern India

The following extract is a description by Kathleen Gough (1959) of Nayar society in the eighteenth century before British rule in India:

> The 'family group' consisted of brothers and sisters, the sisters' children and their daughters' children. The oldest male was the head of the family and the guardian of the children. This was an economic group working and owning property together.

> The men of the Nayar tribe are trained warriors and were often engaged in warlike activities, away from their villages. At such times only the eldest male from each family would remain in the village.
>
> A Nayar girl would go through a ritual marriage ceremony before puberty to a man from a linked kinship group. The ritual husband had no further obligations to her. Her only obligation to him was to carry out rites of mourning for him on his death. The main significance of the ritual was that she was now seen as a 'married woman', who could take 'visiting husbands'. She would take a number of these 'visiting husbands', usually three to eight; they would bring her gifts in return for a sexual relationship, but would not support her. The only obligation a visiting husband had to her was to acknowledge that he was probably the father if she became pregnant, and to give cloth and vegetables to the midwife. She continued to live and bring up her children as part of her mother's kin group, supported by her brothers.

The Nayar clearly do not have a central family structure as we know it. But Gough argues that their family structure nonetheless carried out essential functions.

Post-revolutionary Russia

After the Bolshevik revolution in Russia, an attempt was made to weaken the role of religion in personal life and the domination of women by men perpetuated in family life. To this end, religious marriages were replaced by civil marriages, and divorce made much easier to obtain. A wife was no longer bound to live with her husband, or take his name and discrimination against illegitimate children was made illegal. Nowadays, in the former Soviet Union civil ceremonies are still encouraged, divorce is relatively easy and women are encouraged to take an equal role in work outside the home. Comprehensive nursery and child care are provided by the state to ensure this is possible.

The Kibbutzim of Israel

The Kibbutz was an attempt to create a self-supporting community based on socialist ideals. It was also an attempt to reduce the power and importance of the family in the new Jewish state of Israel, established in Palestine after World War II. The kibbutzim were designed as democratic communities, with all means of production owned by the entire community and policy decided by a number of committees. In order to cope with difficult conditions in the new state, especially the poor agricultural land, all adults had to work.

The links between parents and children was played down and children were brought up in a separate children's house by a 'metapelet', who acted as a nurse, housemother and educator. The children saw their parents each evening for a short period and also at weekends, but returned each night to sleep in the children's house. Parents had only basic facilities in their living quarters – all meals, laundry and so on were provided communally by the kibbutz.

As Israel developed a more affluent Western style economy, developed based on an urban lifestyle with a high standard of living, the social life of the kibbutz also changed. There is now more emphasis on the family unit, and communities have given more priority to the housing needs and living conditions of married couples and their children. The kibbutzim were only ever a small proportion of the total household arrangements in Israel and their numbers have significantly declined.

Exam focus

According to Murdock, who examined 250 different societies, a type of nuclear family existed that was compatible with his definition:

> The family is a social group characterized by common residence, economic cooperation and reproduction. It includes adults of both sexes, at least two of whom maintain a socially approved sexual relationship, and one or more children, own or adopted, of the sexually cohabiting couple (Murdock 1949)

Write a critical assessment of the definition using the material and examples you have read about in this chapter. Aim to structure your material logically and identify which material provides the best means to assess the definition. Write at least one side of A4.

Important concepts

Nuclear • Extended • Patriarchy • Matriarchy • Matrilineal • Patrilineal • Matrilocal • Patrilocal • Endogamy • Exogamy • Socialization • Polygamy • Polyandry • Monogamy • Serial monogamy • Arranged marriage • Malestream • IVF

Critical thinking

1. In what ways do we need to re-think how we understand 'family' in the light of the variations in living arrangements, the family as 'display', and other variations discussed in this chapter?
2. To what extent is the functionalist perspective redundant now? In what ways does the evidence of marital conflict, domestic violence and child abuse contribute to this?
3. In what ways has the role of women changed, both inside and outside the home?

Chapter 3

Consensus Theories of Families and Households

By the end of this chapter you should:

- be able to identify the main differences between structural and action theories, consensus and conflict theories, modernist and postmodernist approaches in sociology
- be familiar with the main elements of functionalist and New Right perspectives
- be able to apply postmodernist criticisms to traditional theories of families and households
- be able to apply theoretical ideas to the family
- be able to evaluate these ideas, using perspectives
- recognize possible changes in the functions of the family
- be able to apply these ideas – and criticisms of them – when you are assessed on them

INTRODUCTION

At the heart of this book – and in all sociological thinking, in general – are sets of competing theories that have many observations to make not only about the study of the family, but also about many, if not all, aspects of social life. This chapter will explore what are generally seen as 'consensus' theories of the family, functionalism and the New Right, whilst Chapter 4 will address more 'conflictful' theories of family life. It is important to recognize that this is not a rigid distinction – consensus theories do address issues of conflict within the family, and vice versa. Neither is this the only way that theoretical divisions could be classified. Traditionally, sociological perspectives are also categorised as either 'social system' (or 'structure'), or 'social action' approaches (or just 'action' approaches). These two approaches emphasize different aspects of social behaviour. The main focus of the 'social system/structural' approach is society and how it operates. The 'social action' approach focuses primarily on people and their lives in society. They may, in fact, look at the same social patterns and behaviour, but they approach them from different angles. These approaches have been part of the traditional theoretical basis of sociology.

In more recent times, perhaps as a reflection of, or in response to the wider social changes that took place at the end of the twentieth century – we have seen the rise of theories that do not quite fit in with either side of this structure–action divide, and some that attempt to bridge it. These include ideas from postmodernism, Michel Foucault and Anthony Giddens.

- Postmodern approaches to the family – such as those adopted by Stacey (1990), Cheal (1993) and Bernardes (1993, 1997) – seek to explain the diverse, fragmented and plural nature of family life, and what the family offers and means to the individual.
- Michel Foucault (1977, 1979, 1985, 1986), an advocate of what we call the 'post-structuralist perspective', views the family as a massive site of control, repression and surveillance on the body. This is a very different image of the family from that offered by functionalism, as described in this chapter.
- Anthony Giddens' structurational project attempts to bridge the divide between 'structure' and 'action'. Giddens (1984) explores the two-way relationship between social actors and the reality in which they act. According to this view, the family is both a ready-made feature of the life into which we are born, and something we help to make through our actions and interactions.

Before we can consider these more up-to-date sociological ideas in detail and delve into the strengths and weaknesses of the functionalist view of the family (a classic example of a purely structuralist sociological approach), we must first consider the terms 'structure' and 'action'.

THE STRUCTURE–ACTION DIVIDE

The social system approach is often called 'structuralist', which means that it concentrates on large-scale social *structures* and social *systems* – how the whole of society (or parts of it) works. It looks, for example, at the role of the family in society: not just one family, but families in general – the family as a social institution. Another object of study is the changing pattern of marriage and divorce in the whole of society over a period of time. This approach emphasizes the power of society over the individual, and shows the way in which the individual's behaviour is constrained and influenced by social forces beyond his or her control – social institutions, norms and roles. In this approach, therefore, it is society that is the most important focus. Society is a system external to the individual but the individual is produced by society, socialized into society's culture, influenced by social groups and institutions, and controlled by society's norms and values.

In contrast, the social action approach of 'interpretive' sociology emphasizes the role of individuals in society and their ability to shape their own social behaviour – the way in which individual people take action. Individuals are aware of themselves and their relationships with others; they have personal motives and interests. Social behaviour has meaning for them, and they interpret situations and actions in terms of their own meanings. When studying the family, advocates of this approach might be more interested in factors such as the *experience* of marriage and divorce, and what this experience means to the couples concerned. The emphasis of this approach is therefore on the individual within society.

The differences between these two approaches do not mean they have nothing in common. They are, of course, both sociological perspectives; both are interested in patterns of social behaviour and there is considerable overlap between them. For example, a sociologist who follows a social action approach would not deny the important influence of society, or believe that individuals behave just as they like, with no reference to others. An interpretive sociologist would recognize the institutions, norms and roles of society, but would see them as the influential context in which action and negotiation take place; the emphasis is still on the action. Similarly, within the systems approach, a structural sociologist would not deny the ability of the individual to make decisions – the image portrayed is not one of human puppets entirely controlled by social forces – but the emphasis is still very much on social structure.

BRIDGING THE STRUCTURE–ACTION DIVIDE

Giddens (1984) argues that theories that look at only one side of the structure–action divide miss the point about the true nature of social life and how sociologists should think about it. Rather than paying lip service to one side whilst firmly rooting his ideas in the other, Giddens seeks to unite both structure and action into what he calls 'structurational sociology'. Culture, of which the family is but a part, is both a constraint from without and made from within. Both sides have to be studied in order to obtain the full picture. This is a major problem with theories such as functionalism, Marxism, feminism and interpretive sociology, as we shall see. Together, they might cover both structure and action, but they do not do so individually – hence, they miss half of the theoretical boat! Equally, on the 'structural' side of the divide, functionalists and Marxists disagree about the true nature of this structure.

TYPES OF 'STRUCTURE': CONSENSUS AND CONFLICT APPROACHES

Within the purely structural approach, there is a clear divide between those who see social behaviour as characterized by consensus and those who see conflict predominating. We have all experienced conflict – situations where we disagree with others, or want different outcomes; most of us have at some time had our wishes blocked by others whose intentions conflicted with our own. On the other hand, sometimes things seem to go much more smoothly; it is easy to see that some aspects of social life do seem to work reasonably well most of the time and life is often easier when there are clear rules or patterns that we know everyone will follow.

These two views of social behaviour are reflected in the two sociological perspectives of consensus and conflict. The consensus view of society concentrates on the way in which society lives in harmony; a harmony based on the fact that everyone has common values and this is seen as essential for a smooth-running social life. Those who see conflict as the predominating characteristic of human society, on the other hand, concentrate on the *differences* of interest that exist between groups in society. They also focus on the role of power and coercion, whereby a dominant group imposes its own values on the rest. The divisions in society are therefore seen as important; this is in great contrast to consensus sociologists, who see the values of society as being common to all members and therefore a strong source of social solidarity.

Ⓐ

Exercise 3.1

We can all see the importance of harmony and consensus in our social lives. However, we can also think of potential sources of conflict. For example, there may be some general agreement as to what household chores should be done by whom, in order to ensure a fair distribution of tasks. However, there may be conflict if, for example, a young person wishes to go out one evening rather than do his or her share of the washing-up. In this case, power and coercion might be brought into play to make the young person conform to the 'consensus' view. We do not always have interests in common. In more extreme cases, a conflict of interests between groups of people might lead to a strike, a riot or even a revolution!

In order to investigate the roles of consensus and conflict in our daily lives, try to think of examples of each in a number of different social situations – for each area of social life, you should try to find two sources/situations of harmony and two sources/situations of conflict. Write your examples in a table copied from the following example:

Situation	**Source of harmony**	**Source of conflict**
Workplace: Employer/employee relations		
Education: Teacher/pupil relations		
Politics: Government/citizen Relations		
Religion: Personal/institutional Issues		

Functionalist sociologists stand in the consensus 'camp', whereas Marxist and feminist sociologists put greater stress on conflict – we shall now turn to the functionalist approach.

FUNCTIONALIST THEORY

Historical context

Functionalism dominated sociology until the late 1960s and has also been a very influential force in anthropology. The French sociologist Emile Durkheim (1938) was a key figure in the development of sociological theory, and functionalism in particular. He was committed to establishing sociology as a credible academic discipline. He saw social order as rooted in a foundation of common core values – the basis of social control and social solidarity.

These ideas were incorporated into the functionalist approach. Durkheim also adapted the work of the philosopher Herbert Spencer (1971) and his ideas on the evolution of society.

The roots of functionalism also lie in the work of anthropologists throughout the twentieth century. When studying small-scale tribal societies, anthropologists have often analyzed aspects of their way of life in terms of how the performance of some practice or ritual might function to maintain the well-being of society.

The following three subsections introduce some of the main concerns of functionalism, in general. Afterwards, we shall look at functionalist theories of the family in more detail.

Consensus and harmony

According to the functionalist view of society, the maintenance of social order is vital, as otherwise there would be anarchy. The basis of this social order lies in a set of shared values. Value consensus means that everyone in society is in agreement about what is important, essential and good. Society can therefore run smoothly on this basis of cooperation. These values run through all parts of the social structure and all social institutions, and thus form an important source of integration for society. In order to ensure that all members adhere to this set of common values, it is also essential that every individual is suitably socialized into sharing them.

Social systems

Functionalists see society as a *system* – a number of parts that together make up a whole. Each part carries out a particular task or function, but each contributes to the efficient working of the whole. This way of looking at a system stems originally from Herbert Spencer's (1971) comparison of society and its functioning with that of a biological organism – that is, a living body. This is known as the 'organic analogy' and it goes as follows. A body or other biological organism is made up of a number of parts. The human body, for instance, has a range of different parts or systems, each of which serves a particular purpose. These parts include the heart and circulatory system, the lungs and respiratory system, the brain and nervous system, and so on. Each part is interrelated with and dependent on the other parts. If we were to remove a heart from a body and place it on a table to be studied, it would stop working – it can only be analyzed as part of a whole system. So, a functionalist analysis of each part looks at the contribution that part makes to the general well-being of the body – how it helps to keep the body 'ticking over'.

Exercise 3.2

Copy and try to complete the following diagram of a body, showing the different organs and systems, and what functions they perform for the maintenance of the body.

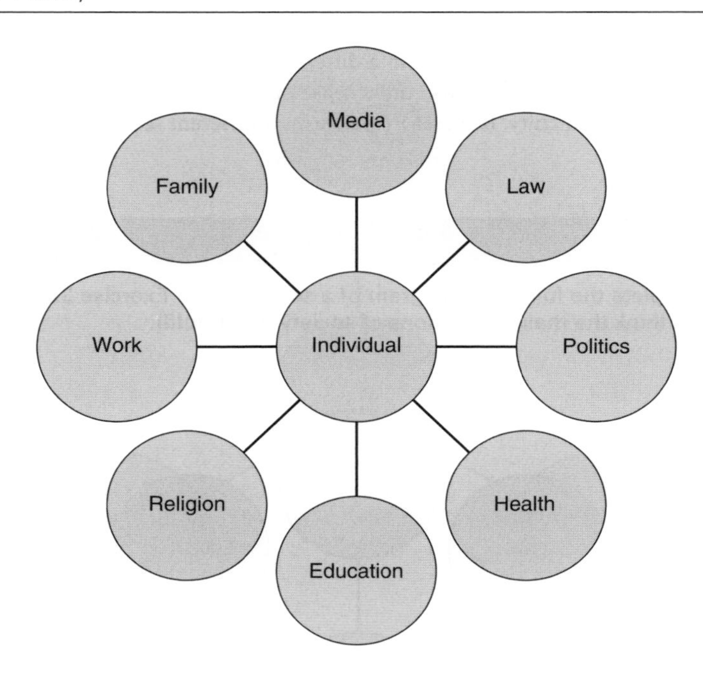

Second, how is this part of society related to the other institutions? In order to answer this question, we need to analyze how one institution – here, the family – serves and influences the other institutions of society. And how, in turn, the family is served and influenced by those other institutions.

Ⓚ Ⓤ Ⓘ Ⓐ

Exercise 3.5

This exercise is designed to encourage you to find some of your own answers to this second question. Copy the following table and then fill in the gaps. Use those already completed to guide you to appropriate answers.

Functional relationships between the family and other social institutions

Institution	Influence *from* family	Influence *on* family
Education	Family socializes child before school and provides support during school years	
Religion		Religion sets down rules for marriage and family relationships Provides family solidarity

Politics	Family provides new socialized citizens/voters and imbues young person with initial political attitudes	
Law		Laws determine boundaries with regard to how family members can treat each other – e.g. the age at which children can be left alone, and so on
Work		Supplies jobs and income to support family members

Equilibrium and change

One of the most frequent criticisms of functionalism is that it does not adequately account for social change: indeed, if all parts of society are fulfilling their purpose or function satisfactorily, then why should there be any need for change? In this respect, functionalism can be viewed as a rather conservative theory – it appears to support the *status quo* (the way things currently are), and therefore other sociologists would say that it supports those who are in power.

However, social change clearly does take place and functionalists have attempted to account for it. In general, they see society as balanced, frictionless, in equilibrium, but recognize that changes will inevitably take place to disturb this equilibrium. Change is, however, usually seen as something that is temporary, a transitory period of adjustment between periods of stability. In the section on historical context, the name of Herbert Spencer was mentioned. Spencer has sometimes been called a 'social Darwinist' because, as did Charles Darwin, he believed in a theory of evolution – but in this case *social* evolution. Spencer believed that, as a society grows and develops, the institutions within it may change in terms of the precise functions they perform and the way in which they perform them, in order to meet the changing needs of society's members and ensure its continued effectiveness.

When studying the sociology of the family, we shall come across a number of theories that depict the family and its structure as responding to changes elsewhere in society – for example, the evolutionary theory of the transition of the family in modern society from an extended to a nuclear structure. Later in this present chapter, we shall see how some functionalist writers talk about a 'loss of functions' by the family, as other institutions have taken over the fulfilment of some of the needs the family used to fulfil in a simpler form. According to these writers, as the family lost these functions, it gradually became more specialized in its remaining functions.

ⒾⒶ

Exercise 3.6

This exercise requires you to investigate the process of adaptation to social change and the way in which it can spread throughout the various institutions in the social system.

Talcott Parsons

Parson's analysis of the family (Parsons and Bales, 1955) can be divided into three parts. He bases each of these on his knowledge of the modern American family:

- basic and irreducible functions
- the modern nuclear family
- complementary roles.

Basic and irreducible functions Parsons believes that every family in every society has two 'basic and irreducible' functions: the *primary socialization of children* and the *stabilization of adult personalities*. The initial or primary socialization takes place in the early years of a child's life within the family group. During this period, the child learns the basic elements of the culture into which she or he has been born. This early stage of socialization is followed by a process of *secondary socialization*, which takes place in more formal groupings outside the family – such as school. The individual *internalizes the society's culture* – that is, the norms, values and customs become so familiar that the individual adheres to them without even thinking about them consciously and they guide his or her actions. Parsons' second aspect of primary socialization within the family is the structuring of personality – the emergence of a personality in the child, focused on the central value of society, such as the motive to achieve.

The second basic and irreducible function is the stabilization of the adult's personality. The family gives the individual adult a 'safety-valve', a place where she or he can relax, escape the stresses and strains of the world outside and feel emotionally secure. The family provides in the home a warm, loving, stable environment where the individual adults can be themselves and even 'let themselves go' in a childish and undignified way. At the same time, the supervision and socialization of children gives parents a sense of stability and responsibility.

The modern nuclear family Parson's ideas about the changes that have taken place in the family and the nature of the modern nuclear family are related to the impact of the process of industrialization. He describes the pre-industrial family as an extended unit that performed many functions for its members and society. With the onset of industrialization, he argues, this type of family was replaced by a nuclear family – a small mobile unit, performing fewer functions but with a more suitable form to fulfil the needs of modern industrial society.

Ⓘ Ⓐ Ⓐⁿ Ⓔ

Exercise 3.8

What sort of functions do you think the pre-industrial family performed? Think about what it needed to do for its members and how far the modern nuclear family carries these out today. Copy and complete the following table:

Changing functions of the family

Traditional family functions	How the family carried them out in the past	How and by whom they are carried out today

Complementary roles Parsons suggests that there is a 'natural' division of labour within the nuclear family. The husband is seen as the *instrumental* male, who goes out into the world to compete and achieve by working and earning money to support his family. This activity produces stress and anxiety for the instrumental male, so he needs to return to a cosy nest, where he is cared for, supported emotionally and understood. The one who caters for these needs is the *expressive* female. In caring for both her husband and her children, she provides warmth, love and security, and relieves the tension caused by the world outside. Parsons sees these two roles as complementary, each providing essential elements of the basic and irreducible functions referred to earlier. Who carries out which role is, according to Parsons, determined by biology – the woman is the one who bears the children, so she should be the one who provides them, and her husband, with nursing, care and support – hence the 'expressive' nature of her role. In the impersonal world of modern life, Parsons sees these roles as very important and the nuclear family as particularly suited to provide them. The nuclear family thus becomes a haven for its members, but a haven that can be easily relocated elsewhere in order to fit the need of modern industrial society for a flexible, mobile workforce.

Ⓚ Ⓤ Ⓐⓝ Ⓔ

Exercise 3.9

To a large extent, Parsons was describing the family that he himself knew – the middle-class American family of the 1950s. To what extent do you believe that his idea of complementary 'instrumental' and 'expressive' roles still applies today? How have things changed in terms of family roles? Certainly, most married women work outside the home, but does this mean that the rest of the marital relationship is more equal?

Copy out the table below and list the responsibilities that are traditionally associated with 'instrumental' and 'expressive' roles. Then decide which of these you feel have changed, and which have changed little in the families with which you are familiar.

	Traditional instrumental (male) responsibilities	**Who is most likely to take these responsibilities today?**
1		
2		
3		
4		
5		
6		
	Traditional expressive (female) responsibilities	**Who is most likely to take these responsibilities today?**
1		
2		

3		
4		
5		
6		

It is worth mentioning at this point that the particular views of the family expressed by Murdock and Parsons were, to a certain extent, a product of the times in which they were writing – the 1950s. Later studies of the family take different views, especially the most recent postmodernist studies, which entirely refute the idea that the family has a single set form, and indeed that, with such a diversity of structures, it cannot be described by one word – 'family' – at all.

However, in recent years New Right theorists have expressed a yearning for the past family form described by Parsons. Their attitude towards the family is very similar to that of the functionalists, and they suggest that the decline and deterioration of the family since that time has led to a host of social problems and increased social disorder. They see the nuclear family as the most 'natural' and 'correct' form, and urge a return to this way of life for all. A more detailed outline of the New Right is provided later.

Ronald Fletcher

Fletcher's contribution to the functionalist theory of the family (1966) has been to analyze the extent to which functions formerly performed by the family have, in modern society, been taken over by other agencies. He assumes that, in the pre-industrial past, the family was a multifunctional unit, performing a wide range of functions for its members and fulfilling all their needs.

He argues that, whilst other agencies have become responsible for six 'non-essential' functions, the family still performs three 'essential' functions that *only* the family can perform. The welfare state and other institutions have relieved the family of its responsibility for the more peripheral functions, but the family carries out its remaining functions in a much more effective and detailed way. Indeed, he argues that the state actually supports the family in fulfilling its essential functions. The essential functions referred to by Fletcher are:

- stable satisfaction of sexual needs
- production and rearing of children
- provision of a home.

With additional support from the state, it is clear that the modern family is able to provide for its members in a far more satisfactory way than previously, so that the family's performance of these functions has improved a great deal. A married couple may be aided by other organizations in the satisfaction of their sexual needs (for instance, through the provision of guidance or contraceptives); they may be aided in their production of children and in the socialization and rearing of these children (for instance, by health clinics, playgroups, speech therapy); and they may be helped to provide an adequate home for their family (for instance, via council housing, grants and rebates).

ⒾⒶ

Exercise 3.10

Copy and complete the following table, showing how the family is helped to carry out its essential functions.

Essential function	What the family does	How it may be helped by other agencies
Stable satisfaction of sexual needs		
Production and rearing of children		
Provision of a home		

Item A

The non-essential functions referred to by Fletcher are:

- economic
- education
- government
- recreation
- religion
- health

He suggests that other organizations have taken over provision in many areas formerly dealt with by the family:

- The family is no longer an economic unit, providing for its own needs.
- It is no longer the sole provider of education – that is, socialization and training for work.
- It is no longer self-governing, with the father holding sway over the other members.
- Recreation is now provided by a mass leisure industry, not within the home.
- Religion is now largely observed in specialized places of worship, rather than being taught in the home.
- Our ailments are now treated by doctors and hospitals, rather than family members.

Clearly, there is a certain degree of validity to these claims. However, as Fletcher argues, the family has not been stripped of all influence and importance – it may still play an important role in each of these areas of life. For instance:

- The family no longer provides for all its own needs; yet, it is still a unit of consumption, consuming goods as a household, rather than as individuals.

- Formal education may take place in schools and colleges, but family support and family preparation for school has been shown to be vital.

The same sorts of argument can be applied to all the areas of life described above.

Ⓘ Ⓐ Ⓐn Ⓔ

Exercise 3.11

Copy the table below and the list of all of Fletcher's 'non-essential' functions (see Item A). Then, for each one write down which institutions seem to have taken them over from the family. Finally, for each one, show how the modern family is still involved in these functions.

Non-essential functions

Function	Taken over by?	How is the family still involved?

An important additional question is how adequately these needs were really catered for in the past. For example, living conditions, diet and health were certainly poorer in pre-industrial Britain. What provision really was made for education and recreation? Fletcher suggests that, nowadays, for both essential and non-essential functions, the family, with the support of the state, provides for the needs of its members in a much more complete and satisfactory way. This picture of an ever-improving modern family has been referred to as the 'march of progress'.

David Popenoe

Neo-functionalists such as Popenoe in the United States have argued that, although there is increasing diversity in family forms in the twentieth and twenty-first centuries, this should not be a cause for celebration, as the negotiation necessary in different family forms is difficult to maintain over the long term to preserve social stability. Popenhoe (1996) accepts that the 'old' family cultural script no longer has any appeal to people, but he draws upon what he sees as biological imperatives to try and establish a new cultural script for the 'new standard family'. This script is based on what he defines as 'biosocial reality', the differences between men and women, so that women are given a traditional role in bringing up children, but only for as long as the children are young enough to need female nurturing. This new standard family is also important because Popenhoe and other neo-functionalists argue that children brought up in alternative family forms are disadvantaged by their early childhood experiences, although this is contested by other American sociologists such as Furstenberg (1999).

Exercise 3.12

Although these functionalist writers vary somewhat in respect of the aspects on which they choose to focus in detail, they all have a number of characteristics in common. We have provided two examples below. You should now think of at least three more similarities.

Similarities between functionalist theories:

- All present a harmonious picture of family life and a positive view, tending to ignore the possible disadvantages.
- Males and females are seen as having different but natural functional roles.

Exercise 3.13

Strengths and weaknesses of the functionalist approach

For this exercise, you are asked to complete the following statements on the main strengths and weaknesses of the functionalist theories. You should try to fill in all the gaps using each of the terms or phrases listed at the end.

Strengths

1. There is a clear recognition of the .... of the family in many societies.
2. Functionalists show how social change may lead to .... in the way social institutions work.
3. The approach illustrates the way in which social institutions can work at both the .... and the .... level – meeting the needs of individual members and maintaining the continuity of the whole society.
4. Functionalists show the .... between society's institutions; they cannot be seen in isolation.
5. The potentially strong relationship between industrial society and the .... is shown.
6. Many .... aspects of the family are revealed.
7. Functionalists show the vital importance of the .... of children into society's culture and the likely role of the family in this.
8. They show how family life may reflect general societal ....

Missing words

- societal
- individual
- positive
- values and norms
- socialization
- adaptations
- nuclear family
- central position and importance
- connections

the whole system. Society operates in the same way a human body does, with each institution having its own role and contributing to the efficient working of the whole system. However, according to Marxists, hard work and determination to succeed are opportunities open only to some people. There is evidence of inequality in the very structure of society which prevents those from the lower social classes being able to gain from hard work and toil. A child born into a poor family will be more likely to suffer poor health, leave school with fewer qualifications, and work in an unskilled job than a child born into the upper class. For Marxists, functionalists essentially fail to acknowledge – let alone explain – the inequalities in opportunities and life chances that exist in a capitalist society. Instead, they adopt the ideological position associated with the beliefs that lie behind the 'American Dream' and use it as the starting point for their analysis of the workings of society.

Important concepts

Consensus • Conflict • Structure • Action • Modernism • Postmodernism • Equilibrium • Structuration • Socialization

Critical thinking

1. Is the traditional functionalist perspective so old that it has little to tell us about the family in the twenty-first century? Or has the New Right modernized an out-of-date theory and applied it appropriately to changes that have taken place?
2. Consider the evidence of child abuse and domestic violence discussed in Chapter 5. How does the picture of harmony and happiness presented by the functionalists fit with this evidence?
3. In what ways could the functionalist perspective and New Right be seen as providing the necessary 'corrective' to the outdated traditional Marxist perspective?

Chapter 4

Conflict Theories of Families and Households

By the end of this chapter you should:

- have gained knowledge on the 'conflict' perspective on the family
- be able to apply Marxist and feminist ideas to the study of the family
- be able to distinguish between different types of feminist sociology
- be able to evaluate Marxist and feminist ideas
- understand the relationship between the family, capitalism and patriarchy
- be able to link these 'conflict' theories into wider debates on the family such as 'Is the family universal?'

INTRODUCTION

Much of the sociology of the family that takes a conflict, radical or critical stance has as its starting point a critical review of functionalist or 'consensus' ideas about the nature and role of the family that we explored in Chapter 3. For many thinkers, the last theoretical nail has been hammered into the coffin of functionalism – its place in contemporary sociological analysis has been lost to other, 'newer' ideas. The battle with functionalism is over and it is time to take stock of the casualties of the fight. Assessing the casualties of the functionalist argument includes updating the 'rosy image' of family life presented by writers such as Murdock (1949), Parsons (Parsons and Bales, 1955) and Fletcher (1966).

The starting point for the battle with functionalism, which overtook much if not most of sociological theorizing in the 1970s, was the development of Marxist and feminist perspectives. Although Marx himself died in 1883, 'Marxism' (in today's sociological usage) did not rise to prominence as a popular sociological tool until much later – the early 1970s. Equally feminist thought did not really become popular in 'mainstream' sociology until the early 1980s. This chapter will begin the task of reassessing functionalism by introducing Marxist and feminist perspectives in general.

THE CONFLICT APPROACH TO SOCIOLOGY

Whereas functionalist theories concentrate on consensus and harmony, other perspectives look at conflict in social life. Whereas Marxism emphasizes class inequality and conflict, feminism seeks to understand the nature of gender inequality and conflict. Key features of many sociological debates are the differences and similarities between the 'consensus' and 'conflict' schools of thought.

Functionalism could be seen as supporting the *status quo* (the way things are) in society by advocating the functional and therefore the so-called 'normal', 'natural' and 'universal' aspects of social life, including the family itself. Many commentators suggest that functionalist views on society in general – and the family in particular – are highly ideological: they are concerned to protect society as it is, to conserve the existing social order. These values are associated with right-wing political ideas. This right-wing ideological bias in functionalist thought is mirrored today in New Right thinking – perhaps showing that sociological theories never go totally out of fashion, they just inform others to come along in their place over time. On the other hand, both Marxism and feminism advocate social change – they seek to readdress what they view as fundamental inequalities in social life. In this way, they have both a sociology and a polity: a way of thinking and a way of acting.

THE MARXIST VIEW OF SOCIETY AND THE FAMILY

For Marx and Engels, the most important feature in all societies is the way in which the economy is organized. In other words, class relationships are the key to understanding social life. For Marx, 'class' as a category is determined by one's relationship to the '*means of production*', the ways in which the economy is organized to deliver the necessities of life – food, clothing, shelter and goods. In a capitalist society, people can own either the means of production and be a member of the capitalist class, or their labour power (the working class), which they sell for wages to those who own the means of production. This relationship underpins every other aspect of life in society, including the nature of the family.

Class conflict between the opposing interests of the capitalist class and the working class is the dynamic that pushes social history towards newer forms of social organization. Marx believed that after capitalism we would see the rise of communism, where the means of production would be collectively or communally owned, thus ending class inequality and therefore class conflict. In this conflict between different class interests, social order is maintained through what Marxists term 'ideology' – ideas that serve to support and protect the interests of the powerful in society (see Chapters 2, 5 and 7). Ideology gives the working masses a state of 'false consciousness', where the present state of social organization is seen as normal and natural. Contemporary Marxists, known as neo-Marxists (the 'new' Marxism), who follow the ideas of Antonio Gramsci (1977, 1978), argue that false consciousness is maintained through 'hegemony' – active consent to one's own domination by a ruling class, where we unquestioningly go along with how the world is and, in doing so, we 'control ourselves' and do not try to change or challenge the social order.

The family and capitalist social order

As with other social institutions – such as religion, the mass media, the state and so on – the family can be seen as serving the interests of those who rule, of those who own the means of production. The basic Marxist view of the family is that it serves as a 'safety valve' – a comfortable release from the oppression and alienation experienced at work – thereby allowing such domination and inequality to continue. In this way, the family serves the interests of capitalism.

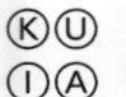

Exercise 4.1

This exercise is designed to test your understanding of what you have read so far in this chapter. When explaining the Marxist and feminist approaches to the family, there are a number of terms you may need to use. Listed below are some of the approaches discussed in the first part of this chapter. You should test your understanding by studying the list of definitions and then allocating the appropriate term to each one.

Terms

- feminism
- economic determinism
- *status quo*
- polity
- social class
- means of production
- capitalism
- communism
- labour power
- false consciousness
- neo-Marxism
- hegemony
- superstructure
- patriarchy
- malestream
- ideology
- consensus

Definitions

1. The idea that people's activities are the product of their economic environment and not their free will.
2. The division of modern society into a hierarchy.
3. A way of examining social life from the viewpoint of women.
4. Control through ideology by the ruling class over the masses.
5. The capacity workers have for work and production.
6. The existing state of affairs.
7. A political unit, normally meaning the state.
8. A type of economy in which production is privately owned and the aim is profit making.
9. A concept used by feminists to describe early sociology, which was dominated by a male view of the world.
10. A set of beliefs imposed by those in power to serve their own interests.
11. The social and cultural activity of society, determined by the economic infrastructure.
12. Ways of thinking (produced by ideology) that hide oppression.
13. Factories and equipment that produce goods and services.
14. A type of society in which males rule and dominate women, both in the family and generally throughout the society.

15. Agreement on the norms and values of society.
16. A political system in which the state has control of production and a monopoly of political power in the name of the people.
17. Attempts to apply Marxist analysis to modern conditions.

The origins of the family: Fredrick Engels

The earliest Marxist answer to the question of the origin of the modern family form is provided by Fredrick Engels (1972) in *The Origin of the Family, Private Property and the State*, first published in Germany in 1884. This text has influenced not only Marxist thought, but also feminist ideas as it traces the origins of female oppression to pre-capitalist economic structures.

This text is understood by some as an exercise in Marxist '*economic determinism*' – the idea that the nature and structure of the economy (referred to as the 'economic base') shapes, directs and determines everything else in society – the 'superstructure'. Engels argues that the origins of today's nuclear family lie in changes made to the nature of private property in traditional society before the onset of industrialization and capitalism. Before humankind had property, the contemporary notion of marriage and family life was not needed – survival was the most important aspect of human life. However, with the rise of private property an organized system of inheritance became necessary – fathers needed to know who their offspring were in order to pass their property down the family line.

With this, argues Engels, the need for monogamy arose – one man married to one woman – and hence the family was created. Therefore, the family serves the interests of the economy – in this case the creation of ownership – whilst subjecting women to unequal power relations in the home. Engels also argues that this was accompanied by the creation of the state – a bureaucratic mechanism to ensure the continuation and legality of marriage and the family.

With regard to the position of women in the household, Engels notes that before industrialization women operated as much in the public sphere outside the home as they did within the private sphere of the family. However, with the early development of an industrial society:

> the wife became the first domestic servant, pushed out of participation in social production . . . she remains excluded from public production and cannot earn anything; and when she wishes to take part in public industry and earn her living independently, she is not in a position to fulfil her family duties. (Engels, 1972: 81)

And

> The modern individual family is based on the open or disguised domestic enslavement of the woman . . . In the family, he [the husband] is the bourgeois; the wife represents the proletariat. (Engels, 1972: 81–2)

For Marxists (and many feminists supporting this view), the family is not the universal, inevitable feature of human life portrayed by the functionalists. Neither is the family a pre-programmed, genetic aspect of human nature, as argued by many biologists and sociobiologists. Instead, it is a human creation: a social invention that has served a specific historical, cultural and economic purpose.

'Is the family universal?' An evaluation of the ideas of Engels

The ideas of Engels have come under much criticism – both within sociology and outside. Although Engels' ideas have been used in Marxist-influenced and some feminist-influenced sociology since the late 1960s and early 1970s to disprove the arguments of functionalism, the evidence can be seen as working both ways. For example, as Murdock (1949) and others have claimed, if the family is an essential feature of all cultures, then can we really argue that it was developed to serve the specific needs of pre-capitalism? Although many societies today are industrialized or industrializing, much of this process is due to globalization and earlier to imperialism and colonialism. In other words, the process of industrialization in non-Western capitalist societies might be seen to be, in some part, due to the ways in which Western societies have managed to force their views onto other societies: through religion, war and the distribution of cultural products – for example, through the mass media. Western capitalism is not, by definition, a global or 'universal' cultural development – so why then is the family, if it is? If the origins of the family, property and the state are all fundamentally linked, why do basic family structures exist in societies that have no experience of the state or property in the Western capitalist sense?

Sociobiologists such as Tiger and Fox (1972) suggested that humans are pre-programmed to engage in communal, familiar patterns of living – an argument in common with the ideas of Morris (1968). Family formation is therefore not the product of economic forces but an essential aspect of being human. Such arguments are, however, difficult to prove: how do you 'see' genetic predisposition? Just because many humans behave in much the same way, to argue that it is natural is a massive presumption.

Exercise 4.2

We have seen how Murdock (1949) described the family as universal because of the functions it performs for society worldwide. Remind yourself of these arguments before using them in the following task.

There is obviously a certain similarity between the work of Murdock and that of Engels, in that they both argue that the family is universal. However, there are also important differences. Write a critical account, comparing the arguments of these two theorists and focusing on each of these aspects in turn:

- the importance of the family to economy or society
- whether the family is an inevitability or a human creation
- Whether women's place in the family is a natural role or female oppression.

at the heart of the alternative 'conflict' perspectives offered by poststructuralism, especially the ideas of French writer Michel Foucault. Foucault (1977) argues that people in society – the masses – are watched and controlled in every aspect of their daily lives – even the so-called 'private' areas of life, such as the family. This 'watching' he refers to as 'surveillance', presenting the image of a 'big brother' society, the term used by novelist George Orwell in his book 1984, where the state exercises control and surveillance over the bodies of women and children in the home, and limits the expression of their sexuality. Discourses (ways of thinking about what is normal and proper) thus define who we are, what we should be and how we should live. They define the 'norm' both within the family and outside in the world of work, and ensure that those who do not conform to this norm are controlled or punished.

The Marxist Jacques Donzelot (1980), who was influenced by the ideas of Foucault, has extended Zaretsky's theme of the 'private' nature of family life. He suggests that the family is not a private aspect of life (even if it appears as such to those who live their daily lives within it). Instead, it is the domain of a complex web of power relations exercised by elites and professionals such as teachers, social workers, doctors, the police and so on, who intervene in family life in a myriad of ways.

Stanley Cohen (1985) is another contemporary writer influenced by the ideas of Foucault. Although not strictly speaking a Marxist, Cohen's sociology is certainly left-of-centre and reflects the ideas raised in this section so far. Cohen suggests that, at the end of the twentieth century, the exercise of social control was very different from the way it was at the start of the century. Cohen seeks to explore, in his words, these new maps, territories and domains of social control, where the individual body is under a massive system of surveillance by a number of different elites. Due to penal policies that involve community care and decarceration, crime and deviance become the concern of the family:

- a 'strong' and 'moral' family upbringing is seen by policy-makers as an essential ingredient of the fight against crime, with parental authority (especially by the father) being vital to this process
- 'deviants' are monitored in the family home, controlled through the day-to-day activities of their own family.

The family is therefore neither private nor a comfort, but very public and a site of massive manipulation. It is interesting to note that these ideas, suggested by Cohen as the new features of social control in the late industrial age, mirror the ideas of the Marxist Donzelot, but are also key features of New Right ideology and the recent policies of New Labour under the direction of Tony Blair.

Strengths and weaknesses of the Marxist approach

Strengths

As with feminism, perhaps the greatest strength of Marxist and Marxist- influenced sociology is that it encourages critical thought about society, rather than seeking to protect and preserve the *status quo*, as functionalism often seeks to do. Advocates of the Marxist approach identify the existence of what they see as fundamental inequalities and power differences in society that result in much of the population (the masses) being controlled by a ruling minority capitalist class in the interests of that class.

With regard to the study of the family, the Marxist contribution has been to suggest that the family – as with other institutions under capitalism – operates to control its members. The key Marxist observation here is that the way the economy is structured (in this case, capitalism) determines the nature of the social and cultural arrangements within society. This observation allows us to consider – as have the writers discussed in this chapter – how and why the ruling class benefits from family arrangements.

However, this emphasis on the large-scale, or 'macro', control and domination by the ruling class of the working class has been criticized by many sociologists. For example, micro-sociologists argue that all social life – including the family – is meaningful to those involved in it, and that individuals do have a degree of free will and independence. We are not always passive victims of control, surveillance and ideology. We do not always live under false consciousness and can often see society for what it is. These claims about the amount of freedom from domination that people may or may not have can be seen as being answered by the neo-Marxist idea of hegemony: the notion that we go along with our own domination because it seems 'natural', even though we are aware of it at the time.

To summarize the strengths of the Marxist approach to the family:

- Marxism offers a critical alternative to more 'consensus' oriented theories – such as functionalism
- the family is not seen as a private place but, rather, the object of wider, controlling, social forces
- the family is seen as supporting and reinforcing the interests of the powerful
- Marxism challenges the notion that the family is universal or natural.

Weaknesses

- the approach is largely Western-centric:
- it is highly deterministic – it reduces all aspects of family life to matters of economic class
- it tends to concentrate on class at the expense of gender.

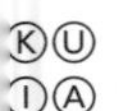

Exercise 4.4

The following passage summarizes the main points of the Marxist view of the family in capitalist society. However, some of the words are missing. Your task is to complete the passage by filling in the gaps with the words listed at the end. The context of each sentence should show you clearly which word belongs in which gap.

> Like the functionalists, Marxists adopt a .... perspective of the family, but see it as dominated by the .... sector. According to Engels, the origins of the family lie in the need to establish a line of inheritance of property. .... marriage was

The family and queer theory

The rise of the family during capitalism has given rise to the notion that a homosexual and lesbian identity could emerge because the system of free labour and the expansion of commodity production created the context for independent personal space to develop. Individual autonomy could develop outside the restrictions and confines of the family. However, Norton (2008) argues that this is an extremely simplistic view and may have been a 'facilitating' factor at most, since documentation of gay subcultures are numerous throughout medieval and Renaissance society – long before the growth of capitalism.

We can identify many attempts to overcome the problem of developing an adequate theory of how patriarchy works – that is, many different feminisms.

Liberal feminism

Liberal feminism – or 'traditional feminism', as it is sometimes known – seeks gender equality through the existing legal structures in society. It does not advocate a radical transformation of gender relations in particular, or across society as a whole.

With regard to the family, a number of liberal feminists have argued that some limited change did take place during the latter half of the twentieth century – a change in the pattern of family roles that indicates a move towards greater equality between men and women. Such claims could be seen as supporting the argument by Young and Willmott (1975) that we now have a more symmetrical family form (see Chapters 6 and 7). In other words, power relations between partners in the home have become or are becoming more equal and both are contributing equally towards domestic tasks in an atmosphere of mutual support and harmony. This situation is said to have developed in recent years and might, if true, be a consequence of changes in women's work patterns and advances in contraceptive technologies, making women more free than ever before.

This claim, however, is the subject of much debate within feminism, as we shall now see. We shall return to this theme in Chapters 5 and 7.

Radical feminism

So-called 'radical feminists' present a very different image of gender relations in society from that proposed by liberal feminists, and very different solutions. Radical feminists blame male biology for gender oppression: patriarchy is seen as 'transhistorical' – it is ever-present in all societies and all cultures. To be a male means dominating women – physically and sexually.

Radical feminism does not, however, represent a unified set of ideas. There are many types of radical feminism, ranging from revolution-inspired theories to lesbian separatism. A classic representation of the radical feminist approach is to be found in *The Dialectic of Sex* by Shulasmith Firestone (1979). Firestone argues that men's power is based on their biology and physical strength, and such power will inevitably underpin and structure all social life, from the socialization of gender roles through to relationships within the family. The pattern of family life we know as the 'nuclear family' is based on male power, and serves to support that power. According to this view, male power is often expressed in the home as physical abuse and violence (see Chapter 5) – a consequence of male biology.

Socialist/Marxist feminism

This view is represented by the work of Michelle Barrett and Mary McIntosh (1982). Within the Marxist-feminist framework, patriarchy is seen as serving the interests of capitalism in much the same ways as those identified by the Marxist Eli Zaretsky. For Barrett and McIntosh, the nuclear family under capitalism is an 'antisocial' family form, as it labels all other forms of family life as inferior and somehow not 'normal'. The only solution to patriarchy within this perspective is a Marxist-style class revolution to bring about a classless society – that is, communism.

Evaluating Marxist feminism: a case for updating?

Although the insights of Marxist feminism are thought have contributed greatly to our understanding of how capitalism and patriarchy work, many thinkers have expressed considerable concern about the way in which it gives capitalism much greater significance than patriarchy. Many other feminists see the Marxist-feminist ideas as 'reductionist' – that is, they reduce patriarchy to a simple causal explanation: capitalism. In other words, class is seen as far more important than gender.

The feminisms discussed in the remainder of this chapter take issue with this Marxist-feminist claim. For example, black feminists are interested in the inter-relationship between ethnicity and gender, whereas dual-systems feminists and, more recently, triple-systems feminists, argue that capitalism and patriarchy are as important as each other.

Black feminism

Authors associated with the recent development of a black feminist perspective have argued that radical and Marxist-feminists have ignored the role that ethnicity and culture can play in female inequality (see Chapter 8). Valerie Amos and Pratibha Parmar (1984) argue that feminist sociologies of the family routinely either ignore the experiences of being black and in a family, or simply trade in white stereotypes about black and Asian life. Many black feminists have made the point that, because they are black, many women experience gender inequality differently from white women, since it is filtered through or combined with their experiences of living in not just a patriarchal society, but also a racist one.

This argument mirrors those of Dallos and Sapsford (1995), who note that the lives of women in African-Caribbean families are often very different from those of women in a white nuclear family: for these black women, the family is much more of a comfort, as it offers protection from the racism of the society surrounding them.

Materialist feminism

Abbott and Wallace (1997) classify the work of French writer Christine Delphy (1984) as 'materialist feminist', although most textbooks categorize Delphy's ideas as 'radical feminist'. As with radical feminists, Delphy argues that sexual oppression is more fundamental than economic class – as defined by Marxists, who are seen as 'sex-blind'. However, Delphy believes that all women share a similar set of social interests due to their common experience of sexual oppression, and therefore that all women constitute a 'class', just as all men form a 'class'. The ideology of the present-day nuclear family, amongst other factors, forces women into 'production' in the form of child-bearing. In other words, childbirth is seen as a biological norm for all women as a class, rather than offering any great freedom of choice. The existence of the family thus supports the 'sexual class' divide between all men and all women by making it seem as though the sexes are fundamentally different by nature, whereas according to Delphy this is ultimately a social construction. The family gives different roles to the different sex partners, thus making 'biological difference' a natural basis for the division of male and female lives and their experiences – first, in the home, but ultimately in the whole of society.

Dual-systems feminism

Whereas Marxist-feminists argue that patriarchy serves capitalism, dual-systems feminists start by making the relationship between capitalism and patriarchy and between the sociological theories of Marxism and feminism more complex. Heidi Hartmann (1979) refers to the relationship between Marxism and feminism as an 'unhappy marriage', since Marxism (as the 'male') dominates and subverts the ideas of feminism (as the 'women'). This unhappy theoretical marriage means that class is seen as the more important subject of analysis and the study of gender is nothing more than an add-on, an optional extra. As Hartmann notes:

> The 'marriage' of Marxism and feminism has been like the marriage of husband and wife depicted in English common law: Marxism and feminism are one, and that one is Marxism. Recent attempts to integrate Marxism and feminism are unsatisfactory to us as feminists because they subsume the feminist struggle into the 'larger' struggle against capital. To continue our simile further, either we need a healthier marriage or we need a divorce. (Hartmann, in Sargent, 1981: 2)

In dual-systems feminism, class and gender interplay with each other. This is not an 'unhappy marriage' as both partners share equally: both class and gender are seen to create inequality and, therefore, sociology should be concerned with the relations between them. Sylvia Walby's earlier works (1986, 1988) demonstrate this dual-systems approach. She argues that patriarchy always coexists with another form of oppression – such as class, under capitalism – although at times the two different forms of exploitation may contradict one another. For example, patriarchy exists in the home through the gendered nature of domestic tasks and male physical power relations – this situation can help to further capitalism by creating the illusion of a happy and emotionally secure private space into which workers can escape. However, the interests of the economy may sometimes be called upon to provide women's part-time labour, taking them out of the home and potentially giving them some economic independence from their patriarchal, home-centred, marriage-centred lives. This happened in Britain during World War II, when women acted as a reserve army of labour to benefit the wartime economy!

Triple-systems feminism

Sylvia Walby's later work (1990) moved on to a 'triple-systems' approach. It is possible to identify six aspects of the structure of patriarchy: six areas of social life that are controlled by men:

- domestic labour, which serves men in the family home and is seen as a 'normal' and 'natural' part of being a woman
- paid work, which segregates women into 'women's work' only
- the state, which promotes a highly ideological image of men, women, marriage and the family, supporting patriarchy in other areas of life, especially through health care, child care and the law
- physical violence by men against women in the home, the workplace and elsewhere
- sexuality, through the highly patriarchal notions of sexuality that are contained within family ideology, and the ideology of 'compulsory heterosexuality'
- culture – familiar and patriarchal ideologies are maintained through cultural institutions such as the media and religion.

Walby seeks to develop an analysis of the lives of women that takes into consideration the fact that class, gender and ethnicity all combine to shape life experiences.

Exercise 4.5

The section to which this exercise relates has discussed the many different 'feminisms' or forms of feminism. You should try to differentiate between them in your own mind. One useful way of doing this is to work out what each sees as the main problem for women and the family in society, and what they offer as the possible answer to that problem. Try to do this in a copy of the table below. You will find the answers in the text, but use your own words.

Type of feminism	What do they see as the main 'problem'?	What is their answer to the problem?
Liberal feminists		
Radical feminists		
Socialist/Marxist feminists		
Black feminists		
Materialist feminists		
Dual-system feminists		
Triple-system feminists		
The New Sexism		

Many feminists would agree that there have been considerable improvements in women's position in society; and equal opportunities legislation from the 1970s has begun, it could be argued, to bring about significant improvements in the position of women. In particular, the role of women in the workforce is now much more accepted – indeed, younger women often put their career aspirations high on their list of priorities. Girls are doing well in school and consistently achieve higher grades than boys in GCSEs and most A-levels subjects. Women now constitute over half of the undergraduate population in universities. The delay in having children has been attributed to middle-class women, in particular, establishing their careers before thinking about becoming mothers. These changes were heralded by post-feminist writers such as Naomi Wolf, who coined the term 'genderquake' to describe the dramatic processes that seemed to indicate that full equality with men was just around the corner.

However, these advances do not seem to apply to all women and this would be a major criticism of the sweeping statements made in this chapter. When we break down the statistics and factual evidence for the advancement of women, we find that working-class women and women from particular ethnic backgrounds do not have the same level of opportunity as white, middle-class women. Women in general still earn approximately three-quarters of what men earn and they are overwhelmingly segregated into low-paid jobs in retail, catering, cleaning and caring professions. Furthermore, once women have children their position reverts to one that would not be dissimilar to the role women played in the postwar period – they take responsibility for most of the domestic labour, child care and routine duties associated with being a wife and mother, whilst men become the 'breadwinner'. Women's dominance in the part-time employment sector further develops the characteristics of their traditional role.

A new type of sexism seems to be emerging. First, related to all the 'evidence' that seems to point to women having achieved equality of opportunity with men, an argument has been presented that there is no need to pursue equal opportunities further because most of the major battles have been won. Women, it is argued, can '*have it all*' – career, family, independence, and choice in all aspects of their lives. This view often portrays feminists who still seek and demand improvements in women's lives in a negative way, putting forward the notion that their perspective is unreasonable and should not be taken seriously. The view also presents feminist perspectives as not typical of what most women aspire to and, therefore, unrepresentative of women generally.

Second – and somewhat more sinister – is the notion that women can express their sexuality freely. If we consider the images we still often see of women in the media, there is a 'traditional' underlying perspective about how women – and, in particular, young women and girls – should behave and present themselves that is explicitly sexualized. Part of the new sexism and post-feminist ideas is the emphasis on the individual self-empowerment whereby young women in particular seem to be more confident, especially about their sexuality. Hence, objections to the overly sexualized portrayal of women's bodies in adverts or men's magazines, the increase in numbers of lap-dancing clubs, beauty pageants, seem to be out of step with 'advancements' women have made, This is perhaps to ignore that pornography is still very much at the heart of the way society perceives of and controls women. Andrea Dworkin has argued that pornography is at the centre of female oppression and the source of all other aspects of female subjugation.

The publication of Helen Sweeting's 19-year-long study of an area of the west of Scotland concludes that, over two decades, teenage girls across all social strata are reporting mental health disorders at a rate of 44 per cent (Hill 2010). Although there have been some critics of this study who have pointed to its limited geographical location, there is also other research that concluded that low self-esteem, anxiety, psychological distress and depression are part of the territory for many teenage girls, despite the commonly held view that their opportunities and personal freedoms have dramatically improved. Government research by Dr Alison Tedston, Head of Nutrition at the Food Standards Agency (Tedstone 2009) has also highlighted teenage girls as a vulnerable group regarding the choices they are making about diet, lifestyle and other health-related issues – which are consistently damaging to their health and outlook.

Walter (2010) argues that despite her earlier views about the success of feminism she now believes that the language of 'empowerment' has been turned from meaning sexual liberation to be associated with sexual objectification. The growth in the use of women's bodies as objects, particularly within the world of celebrity, has led to girls and women increasingly to value themselves only in terms of their physical attributes, and these are the ones that are most closely associated with a male chauvinist or pornographic perspective of women. The world of the hyper-sexualized view of women – super-skinny, super-sexy, super-brainy, together with the rapid growth of the beauty and style industries, has shaped the narcissistic expectations of modern women (Hill 2010). The Coalition government formed after the 2010 election is seeking to protect children from the 'sexualized' media world in its outline of policy initiatives on the family.

Whilst some areas of women's lives have clearly benefited from equal opportunities legislation, other areas have reverted to traditional notions of what a women should be, particularly in relation to the physical and sexual imagery surrounding their status in society and in industries such as the music and the media.

Strengths and weaknesses of the feminist approach

For many sociologists, the ideas of feminism are useful to sociology because of their critical or radical approach to thinking about society and the family. For these sociologists, functionalism is too simplistic and assumes that society is in balance and harmony. Perhaps the greatest contribution made by feminism in general is what is called the 'malestream criticism' of traditional sociology, the idea that women as a social group have been invisible in sociological study and that this is unacceptable. The desire to make women visible has led to a way of thinking about the nature of family life that takes issue with family ideology and suggests that there is no 'natural' way for humans to live their lives – only different cultural traditions.

Strengths

- unlike some versions of Marxism, feminism concentrates on the role played by the family in supporting patriarchy
- as with Marxism – and in opposition to functionalism – feminists see the 'universality' of the family as merely ideology, not reality
- feminists have pointed to a 'dark side' of family life (see Chapter 5) that involves violence and abuse
- feminists have noted that power relations within the home are unequal between men and women (see Chapter 7).

Weaknesses

Although some of the more recent development in feminist thinking – such as black feminism – have begun to take account of the variations between families, the traditional approaches were not particularly sensitive to the pluralism that exists in forms of the family, households or family relationships. What has become known as 'difference feminism' (Somerville 2000) challenges the notion that, in general, the family disadvantages women and is of benefit mainly to men and capitalism. Difference feminists criticize this as failing to take account of how the range and variety of family arrangements have a range of effects on the family lives of women. Women live in a wide variety of household arrangements that will have an affect upon their identity, position in society, definition of themselves and so on. Similarly, single parents who are women cannot be seen as a single category. They may be temporarily single, in a variety of economic circumstances – working, non-working, of different ages, from different socio-economic, ethnic and cultural backgrounds – and all of these aspects will influence their situation and position in society.

This way of 'de-constructing' the nature of family life for women is closely linked with postmodernism, which we will consider later in this chapter. As Bradley (1996) and others have argued when we posed the questions 'What is a "family"' or 'What is a "woman"', we begin to get to the heart of the historically, socially and essentially relativist construction of these categories that have been taken for granted in much of sociology and feminist thinking. Bradley argues that such categories should be overthrown to reveal the ways in which we re-align ourselves as members of other categories at different ages in our life-course. Similarly, we experience many different types of family, household and kinship patterns during our life-course.

Ⓘ Ⓐ Ⓐn Ⓔ

Exercise 4.6

If Marxists see workers as oppressed, in what ways do feminists see women as 'doubly oppressed'? Your task is to describe the ways in which women are oppressed. Write a paragraph about each of the following aspects of women's oppression, describing how they are oppressed by the economic system and by men:

- socialization into the mother/housewife role
- gender inequalities seen as 'normal'
- patriarchy
- women in the workforce – seen as cheap, extra, temporary workers
- false consciousness.

Evaluating feminism: towards post-feminism?

Some contemporary thinkers suggest that feminist analysis – be it of the family, or other areas of social life – has simply gone too far: feminists have overestimated the extent of female inequality in order to further their own political agendas. This opinion is certainly a feature of much New Right thinking (and of some New Left ideas), seeing feminism as an attack on 'traditional family values', which are vital for the moral well-being of an ordered society.

Catherine Hakim (1995) suggests that times have changed and women do have the equality they desired a few years ago: hence, the feminist project has become outdated and is no longer relevant. She believes that women are able to make free and rational choices about their own lives. According to Hakim, women want children, marriage and to engage in domestic labour. Accordingly, they take part-time employment so that they can continue to carry out domestic tasks for their family. If they did not want this, they would not do it.

This argument takes us full circle: is the ideology of the family in common-sense thought true, or is it simply seen to be true within the socially constructed reality in which we live? Are women's (and men's) family lives the product of free choice, nature or simply tradition, and how can we tell?

K I An E

Exercise 4.7

In this section, it has been suggested that women's lives are now filled with free choice, rather than being dominated by patriarchy. To what extent do you think women have acquired equality with men? Carry out some research on the extent to which this is true. You may find ideas in sociology (and perhaps history) textbooks, in newspapers or on TV. You may also gain some useful ideas from older friends or members of your family. You should look for information to fill in the boxes in a copy of the table below. The left-hand column lists a number of different areas of social life. In the second column, you should insert examples of ways in which women have gained ground in terms of rights, status, behaviour and so on. In the third column, you should insert any examples you can find of gender inequalities that still exist.

Area of social life	Gains made by women	Inequalities still existing
Home		
Education		
Health		
Work		
Leisure		
Religion		
Politics		
Legal rights		

MODERNISM, POSTMODERNISM AND THE FAMILY

Much of what is contained in the sociological theories of the family and households we have looked at so far is derived from modernism, according to postmodernists. Modern society or modernity refers to the nature of social relations from around the period of the Enlightenment of the sixteenth and seventeenth centuries until far into the twentieth century. The dominant features of this era were associated with the growth of capitalist practices in the economy and the use of technological innovation, the spread of centralized governmental practice, and the notion of the nation state and democratic political parties. As well as these changes in society, dominant thinking patterns were changing also, embracing technical and scientific knowledge over religious and traditional views and values. Functionalism, Marxism and some aspects of early feminist thought have been seen as products of this particular period of history that has become known as 'modernism'.

These perspectives are characterized by 'grand stories' – that is, they view society as a whole entity that can be explained and understood in terms of patterns and trends in their development, progress and continuity. There is also the underlying belief or assumption made by these perspectives that, in using empirical evidence, the truth about the reality of the world can be revealed. The modernist world was also seen as a time of more personal certainties in terms of the development of our identities; the community in which we were rooted; our place within the economic, political and cultural spheres of life. The 'family' was a central point of certainty where we would develop our roles and identities in life and, using our experience, go on to recreate our own families in the future. Much of the sociology of the family is contextualized within this modernist epistemology and, even though there is significant criticism of the traditional functionalist views of the family, conflict perspectives do not ultimately challenge the overall discourse.

Hence, according to postmodernists most, if not all, features of modernity have disappeared. Economic and employment relations have changed dramatically – production processes are part of a global economy, working life is ever-changing, no one can expect to do the same job for their whole working life. Politically and culturally, we are moving away from nationalism and state responsibility to privatization and personal responsibility. There are no certainties in terms of art, style, identity or a common way of life.

The postmodern perspective has challenged traditional perspectives on the family and identifies a more individualist or pluralist approach to what the family means. Family life has become changing and diverse in the postmodern age. What does it mean to be a family? It would be unwise to view one type of family as more desirable or acceptable than others. In the postmodern era, individuals can choose the type of family and role(s) they play within them according to what suits them best at any one time during their life-course. Work by Beck-Gernsheim (2002) and earlier work by Giddens (1992) focused on the changing meanings and practices of family relationships, and the ways in which love and intimacy are being experienced differently to traditional norms and mores. Giddens identified gay and lesbian couples as pioneers of 'plastic sexuality', whereby sexual relationships were freed from the reproductive process. He also discussed 'pure relationships' becoming the norm as a result of 'de-traditionalisation', by which he meant that, since tradition had declined, people were free to make choices about relationships without external forces holding their relationships together. Relationships were held together by the commitment of the couple to them, rather than pressure from extended family, religion, politics or the economy.

Other writers (Stacey 2002) identified non-standard intimacies and 'families of choice' whereby networks of friends and extra-marital relationships became considered as 'family'. The heterosexual co-resident couple and their children, according to Roseneil and Budgeon (2004), no longer occupied the centre ground, or were the 'basic unit' of most Western societies. The rise in the divorce rate and the number of reconstituted families, single parenthood by choice, births outside marriage; the high proportion of children brought up by a lone parent, single-person households; and the increasing number of childless couples by choice were all testaments to this change in family life. Looking at these points critically, it may be argued that there has always been diversity and change in the composition of families and households, and that many of the features of current family life existed in the past but were simply hidden from view – such as illegitimacy. Another dimension of family change is what has become called the 'reproductive revolution', whereby increasing number of couples seek IVF treatment in order to conceive a child, and where children are born to parents who are not their biological relations. Adoption rates among gay couples also increased to about 130 per annum according to the Office for National Statistics published in 2009, suggesting that non-standard families are increasingly accepted as suitable for raising children.

Is post-feminism postmodern?

To a certain extent, the views of Hakim (1995) are similar to those of feminists who have been influenced by postmodern ideas. Unlike what might be called 'victim feminism', where women are portrayed as helpless victims of male oppression, postmodern feminism seeks to explore the ways in which women's (and men's) lives have opened up and become freer with the onset of choice, diversity and fragmentation of gender roles in the broader postmodernization of society. Although Hakim is certainly not a postmodernist, her ideas can be seen as similar to those of postmodernism, in that she emphasizes the free will that women are able to exercise in the construction of their daily lives.

For example, Judith Stacey (1990) has suggested that contemporary family diversity has opened up a great deal of choice for women: family structures have changed and are still changing, divorce is more commonplace than ever before – as are illegitimacy, homosexuality and cohabitation. In this climate of diversity and choice, argues Stacey, we can also see a form of liberation.

RECENT SOCIOLOGICAL APPROACHES TO THE STUDY OF THE FAMILY, PERSONAL LIFE AND SOCIAL CHANGE

There have been important developments in several sub-fields of the sociology of gender and family. Earlier fields of study – such as the focus on family and community in the research of Young and Willmott (1975) – have given way to research relating to social changes in the family and gender relations, and emphases placed on difference and diversity in household structure. Early feminist attention, which focused on unequal divisions of labour and care in the family, has changed to a concern to study divorce, cohabitation and the reconstitution of relationships. The concept of the 'family' itself has become problematic with increasing levels of breakdown, reordering, and the assumption of the 'heteronormative' framework increasingly challenged in light of same-sex marriage and adoption.

The work of writers such as Roseneil and Budgeon (2004) has provided a significant challenge to the scope of earlier research. Whilst recognizing that the family is still a powerful institution with strong emotional and political controls over us, they argue that sociologists should 'decentre' the family and, in particular, the heterosexual couple in our imaginations. The notion of and focus on the heterosexual couple within a nuclear family with children is the norm for most sociological work in this area. This sidelines or completely ignores 'non-standard intimacies' or 'families of choice', where networks of friends are particularly important for gay men and lesbians (Roseneil 2000).

According to Charles *et al.* (2008), the changes in how we 'do' family in the last 50 years has led to two broad theoretical explanations in sociology. First, the family is being undermined by the process of individualization and 'de-traditionalization' and, second (and conversely), that the changes are leading to greater degrees of equality and intimacy

Chapter 5

Ideology, Discourse and the 'Dark Side' of Family Life

By the end of this chapter you should:

- be able to evaluate the idea of 'family ideology'
- be able to evaluate functionalist images of the family
- have knowledge of critical views of the family other than Marxism and feminism
- have knowledge of recent developments in family sociology emanating from the ideas of Michel Foucault
- be able to apply the idea of the dark side of the family to evidence on abuse in the family
- be able to apply ideas of the dark side of family life to assessment requirements that require discussion of roles, relationships and power in the home in general
- have the knowledge to answer the questions on the dark side of family life given at the end of the chapter

INTRODUCTION

Functionalists such as Talcott Parsons (Parsons and Bales 1955), and the New Right (Scruton 1990), have presented an image of a happy, warm, caring and functional family, or what the family should be. Conservative governments have introduced legislation that has supported conventional family life. Major's 'Back to Basics' campaign in the 1990s, in particular, was part of a 'moral panic' (Lister 1996), where the media and the public become increasingly concerned about the negative effects of an issue – such as family breakdown and single parenthood – which spectacularly backfired after revelations about the private lives of some cabinet ministers revealed extra-marital affairs and illegitimate children. This is also the image we are given by the media – a 'cornflake family' sitting around the breakfast table, laughing, sharing and caring, with mum cooking the meals for dad and their polite, energetic and slightly cheeky kids. To some extent, Marxists such as Zaretsky also saw the family as a haven to escape to from the harsh capitalist world. The question is, is this really what family life is like? Is this image of the family an ideal, or is it simply an impossible dream for those individuals for whom family life causes feelings of being trapped, captive and fearful? This image is part of the wider ideology of the family that stresses the positive side of family life for individuals and society.

We can see from media reports and critical sociological research (Dobash and Dobash 1998, 2000), however, that the family has a 'dark side' – the family can be dysfunctional both for its members and for wider society.

THE DARK SIDE OF FAMILY LIFE AND WHY SOCIOLOGY WISHES TO INVESTIGATE IT

The problem for sociologists interested in family life is that such a private sphere of human activity is difficult to study, yet it is a vital aspect of human societies for a number of reasons:

- the majority of people in the world is believed to live in some form of social organization that we can call a 'family', 'household' or has 'family relationships'
- the family introduces new members of society at birth and is therefore responsible for primary socialization – a key factor in training actors to take part in the adult world
- a great many other social institutions inter-relate with the family, such as educational, health care and religious institutions, the media and so on
- family relationships – especially in the immediate household – are the relationships we experience most in ordinary day-to-day life
- in the eyes of many politicians and religious figures, the family is a special social organization
- the media often create a 'moral panic' about problems in family life and about the so-called 'collapse' of family life in recent years
- the media tend to report 'newsworthy' stories about abuse, violence, death in families.

Therefore, although the family is a difficult topic to study, it is one which deserves sociological study, since it is a major feature of our lives. The family has also been a fundamental area of study for sociologists such as early researchers Young and Willmott in the 1950s. Another reason why the family deserves the attention of sociological inquiry is that, for many, its ideological 'happy image' is far from true. Many claim that, in reality, families create problems for the individual – problems that are largely ignored in early functionalist analyses of the family and hidden by the ideology of the family in society itself.

Ann Oakley

In her books *The Sociology of Housework* (1974a) and *Housewife* (1974b), Ann Oakley claims that, although invisible from the outside, women's unpaid domestic labour should be seen in the same way as paid labour – it is just as time-consuming and demanding. In a similar theme to that expressed by Gavron (1966), Oakley suggests that the alienation, boredom, frustration and helplessness felt by working-class males at work are similar emotions to those experienced by 'housewives' in the family home. Oakley also challenged the 'malestream' nature of sociology and sociological research itself in the 1970s and beyond as failing to include women and/or treating women stereotypically. Oakley's research, which continued over more than 30 years, represented a considerable attempt to redress the imbalance by studying sex and gender, childbirth, and motherhood, culminating in the publication of the *Ann Oakley Reader: Gender, Women and Social Science* (2005), which provided a valuable commentary and overview of her lifelong research. Oakley must also be acknowledged for her approach to feminist research and her critique of conventional sociological research methodologies. Oakley argued strongly that being empathetic towards the subjects of your research gained much more in depth and valuable data than the traditionally positivistic approach adopted by male researchers in sociology.

From these two feminists' points of view, the 'ideology of romance' and the 'ideology of the family' does have a dark side for many married women: the dark side of captivity to domestic chores.

Ⓚ Ⓤ Ⓘ Ⓐ

Exercise 5.3

According to Gavron and Oakley, young women expect romance, freedom and equality in marriage, but these are often not forthcoming. In order to explore this issue more fully, answer the following questions.

1. Why do today's women have higher expectations of marriage than women of previous generations?
2. How well does the 'ideology of romance' prepare young women for the reality of marriage?
3. List the range of activities and skills a young wife/mother is expected to be 'good at'.
4. Explain why Gavron and Oakley often use words such as 'captivity', 'confined', 'trapped' and 'imprisoned'.

Ⓘ Ⓐ Ⓐⓝ

Exercise 5.4

According to Ann Oakley (1974a), housework can be as 'alienating' as routine factory work. The table below contains a list of the main ways in which sociologists describe some types of factory work as alienating. Copy the table and in the right-hand column give examples of ways in which housework might be said to have the same characteristics.

Aspect of alienation at work	Application to housework
Lack of control – over deadlines, nature of work, decision making, skill and judgement	
Lack of meaning and sense of purpose – work is routine and repetitive, product always the same, work is fragmented, no end product with which worker can identify	
Lack of social integration – few opportunities to socialise, lack of cooperation and consultation with others	
Lack of identification with work – work does not feel fulfilling and worthwhile, hostility towards work, reason for work is extrinsic – not in the work itself but outside	

RADICAL PSYCHIATRY

This approach is usually associated with three writers from the 1960s: Edmund Leach, R.D. Laing and David Cooper. Laing and Cooper were originally psychiatrists, but they were to reject many of their ideas for a more society-centred approach termed 'anti-psychiatry', or, as we shall refer to it here, 'radical psychiatry'.

Living in 'a runaway world'

Edmund Leach's book *A Runaway World?* (1967) suggests that, in the isolated nuclear family, there is too much emotional pressure on its members because isolation from other kin causes relationships within the family to become strained and tense. Leach sees this as a particular problem of the modern, industrialized world, where some family members may have to change their geographical location because of work commitments and, in doing so, they isolate themselves from kin who could help them get through times of pressure and tension. Leach's arguments stand in contrast to the home-centred, 'rosy image' that can be found in the work of later sociologists – such as Young and Willmott (1975).

'Madness and the family'

R.D. Laing (1976; Laing and Esterson, 1970) has argued that the nuclear family, a prime area of emotional pressure and anxiety, is a major contributory factor in the development of mental illness – in particular, schizophrenia. For example, we may feel under pressure to act towards some family members in a very different way from others: one adult parent may have different rules compared with another, and so on. In acting out these different

Donzelot (1980) (see Chapter 4). For Foucault, social control is characterized by two vital mechanisms.

Body, discipline and surveillance

Foucault argues that we can chart a common history from the workhouse of the poor in Europe at the beginning of industrialization, through the factory and up to and including the modern asylum, hospital, school and prison. This common history reflects a concern in society to monitor the human body: to limit physical movement over time and between places.

> the body is directly involved in a political field; power relations have an immediate hold upon it; they invest it, mark it, train it, torture it, force it to carry out tasks, to perform ceremonies, to emit signs. (Foucault, 1977: 25)

For Foucault, then, power in society is the ability to be controlled – to have one's actions dictated to one – and, therefore, the individual body is the object of all power struggles.

Foucault seeks to rewrite the history of punishment. He notes that we are told by various ideologies of 'progress' that the modern age is much more civilized and humane than before. The scaffold (torture, hanging, the guillotine) has been replaced by prison, where the criminal is re-educated – loss of liberty being in the best interests of both the population and the offender. However, for Foucault, such a common-sense history of discipline and punishment ignores the fact that increasingly more and more of our daily life is subject to control by the state – our bodies are now subjected to a much more hidden form of control through doctors, teachers and even the family itself. For example, if we consider the basic similarities between the prison, the school and the hospital, as argued by Foucault, we can see that all three of these institutions are concerned with the control of the body: individuals are told where to be, when, and what they should do with their bodies when they are there!

Foucault refers to these modern forms of control as a 'gentle way in punishment' since they do not really involve violence or torture. For example, teachers are not allowed to hit children, and neither should parents – even in the 'private' family home. However, Foucault's use of the term 'gentle' is deliberately ironic: he is suggesting that, although they might seem more humane and gentle, modern forms of control are as powerful – if not more so – than previous forms.

Foucault identifies a number of techniques that are used to make 'docile bodies' in the modern age, to control and limit the actions of the individual:

- *enclosure* – spaces or places are set aside for specific actions
- *partitioning* – individuals are put into their own place in relation to other individuals
- *functional sites* – architecture is used to limit and control movement and actions
- *rank* – individuals are placed within a network of different ranks, they are judged in relation to others.

Underpinning all of these techniques of control is the 'timetable', which allows surveillance to take place. Individuals are controlled in relation to a specific order of events. This is true, argues Foucault, of schools, hospitals, army barracks, asylums, factories, prisons and so on.

This 'watching of movements' – or to use Foucault's term, 'surveillance' – also occurs in the family, and it occurs in relation to a timetable of covenants enforced upon young children by adults (i.e. bedtimes, mealtimes, when they can and cannot watch TV, what rooms they can and cannot enter, and so on). This surveillance of the body is a key feature of the family, especially the control and limiting of sexual expression – of both children and adult married partners.

Foucault also notes that such is the power of this control by surveillance that we – the individual – can operate self-surveillance: we 'learn' (are told!) that some actions are deviant, wrong and so on, and that it is correct, normal and proper that we do not behave in this way. These values are carried around by us as individuals and they guide what we do when we are not being watched by others. We thus control our own body in accordance with the ideas of others. In the family, young children may not act as they wish – even in the so-called privacy of their own room – because they have been taught that some actions are wrong. Equally, adults in a marriage may not act as they wish in the privacy of their own family home because they are worried that wider society may think that their actions are 'deviant', even though these actions take place behind closed doors. These adults may worry about what their friends will think, what the neighbours might say, and how the state might control them through the local police force!

Power/knowledge

The second key ingredient of power in society, according to Foucault, is the existence of what he calls 'power/knowledge'. Foucault makes the point that the control and ownership of knowledge is a prime aspect of power: the power to control and limit others, the power to exercise surveillance over them and to discipline them.

Power/knowledge is exercised through 'discourses' – sets of languages and ways of thinking about the world. Discourses are associated with the spaces or 'sites of power' over which and within which they operate. For example, the discourse – or, rather, the 'technical set of language and knowledge' – that controls the school is pedagogy. The prison is similarly controlled by penology, the asylum by psychiatry and so on. These sets of knowledge dictate what is normal and deviant, how we should and should not behave, what we should and should not do with and to our bodies and when. These sets of knowledge set the timetable that controls our bodies and they give some people the right to engage in surveillance over us.

The family is a major site or 'place' for the operation of powerful discourses on the body. For example, Foucault notes that medical, scientific and religious discourses seek to regulate the 'body of society' – the population, and they do this by focusing on the social institution where all bodies can be found at one time or another – the so-called 'private family'. A good example of how the body is controlled in the family home is provided by social attitudes towards sex and sexuality.

As David Morgan (1985) points out, Foucault questions the existence of 'sexual liberation' in both society and the family. We are still subject to a great deal of sexual control and repression – controlled through discourses on sex. Morgan and Foucault suggest that a process of 'medicalization' has taken place in society: an increase in the medical profession's power over previously non-medical matters. We might be more open in our discussions of sexual matters, but the medicalization of sex ensures that so-called 'normal' standards still hold. This medicalization of sex is related to the medicalization of the family or 'partner relationships': the traditional site for safe sex to be practised.

For Foucault, given the degree of power some in the family have over others, and the power the state has over the so-called 'private home', the family must be seen as a place of control, discipline and punishment: a huge dark side that is often ignored and obscured by the various ideologies of the family that exist in society.

ⓀⓊ ⒾⒶ

Exercise 5.6

When discussing Foucault's main arguments about sexuality, David Morgan (1985) stresses the way in which Foucault uncovers the superficiality of modern liberation in sexual matters. Whilst control over sexual matters seems to be less restrictive, there have emerged new standards of sexual fulfilment and performance. We now seem to be obliged to 'do well' at sex, and the failure to do so is often interpreted as a social or medical problem. A whole range of experts, counsellors, magazines and manuals have emerged for us to consult about our supposed problems in this area.

1. Make a list of sexual problems that might lead to consultation with doctor, therapist or counsellor – problem pages in magazines are a good place to find examples!
2. Use this list to produce an account of the way in which new standards for and expectations about sex are established and disseminated.

Bryan Turner (1984) identifies a common theoretical link between Max Weber's and Michel Foucault's thinking about the family. In *The Protestant Ethic and the Spirit of Capitalism* (1930), originally published in 1905, Weber argues that, with industrialization and the onset of 'modernity', the disciplinary practices of the monastery were transferred to the factory and the family. Through Protestant values, the body is controlled for the 'calling' of God, by limiting food intake and sexual desire. Family members exercised control over their own bodies in regulation with such religious discourses.

However, with the further progress of industrialization and modernity there arose what Weber describes as a 'disenchanted world', caused by the dominance of 'the spirit of capitalism', where individual action is regulated to the smallest degree, both in the factory by the owners and in the home through the bureaucratic mechanisms of the state intruding further into the now not so private family lives. For example, although we think of our family home as private, the state has the right to stop adults from participating in some forms of sexual behaviour, stop parents from hitting their children and stop one adult partner from abusing the other. It has even been suggested that parents might be made by law to operate a curfew, whereby children would not be allowed to go out alone after a specific time. If these dictates were not followed, then representatives of the state would have the right to force their way into the so-called 'private home' and arrest the transgressors.

ⒾⒶ **Exercise 5.7**

We have seen how Michel Foucault sees the 'surveillance of the body' as a key feature of the family, especially the control and limitation of sexual expression. This surveillance, and the exercise of power and knowledge, can be particularly seen in the relationship between parents and their children. Try to think of some specific ways in which this happens in a family situation. Imagine a young child aged, say, seven years. How do parents, or those acting as parents, control him or her in terms of limiting physical movement, controlling the body and determining the way in which behaviour and knowledge are controlled or passed on? Some of the areas of behaviour and knowledge you might consider are sex, travel, dress, play, sleeping, eating and so on.

Evaluating the work of Michel Foucault

For many, the advantages or strengths of Foucault's ideas are that they allow us to develop a new framework with which to think about aspects of society that we previously took for granted. This could be seen as the true value of all good sociology. Foucault asks us not to take for granted what the powerful tell us about why and how they govern over us, but to think about so-called 'humane', 'gentle' and 'liberating' social developments, and to ask 'who benefits?' and 'how might this be a force of control?'

When looking at how power and control operate in society, Foucault gives us a rather dark and subversive image of a society that is subject to extensive control, discipline and surveillance. Many Marxist-influenced thinkers and some feminists have used these ideas to try to explain why inequality continues. Others, such as the New Right, however, might argue that such control is necessary for the well-being of society, or that it is largely a figment of Foucault's imagination: the contemporary age, they would argue, is clearly more liberating than previous ages.

More micro sociologists might suggest that Foucault is far too deterministic in his assumptions about human nature. We might gain the impression from reading Foucault that we have no choice in our domination – that we have no free will to fight against discourses. This idea would be found objectionable by interpretive sociologists, as they tend to emphasize the active and free nature of social action and interaction.

In Foucault's defence, whilst he sees discourses as real and important, he also recognizes that small-scale, localized power struggles can operate within them – giving individuals the opportunity to fight, resist and subvert:

> I do not think that it is possible to say that one thing is of the order of 'liberation' and another is of the order of 'oppression'... one should still take into account – and this is not generally acknowledged... [that] no matter how terrifying a given system may be, there always remain the possibilities of resistance, disobedience, and oppositional groupings. (Foucault, 1984: 245)

Therefore, all discourses provide us with opportunities – the opportunity to fight or to give in: to be controlled or to resist. For Foucault, freedom or liberation from control cannot happen if there is no control to fight against in the first place.

THE POSTMODERN FAMILY?

We might argue that the contemporary family is a postmodern family. Whereas, in modernity, society was optimistic about the role that science and medicine could play in the 'improvement' of family life and sexual behaviour, in postmodernity we have become increasingly sceptical about the intrusion of these discourses into our once private lives. In other words, more and more people have begun to think that state control is unwarranted and unreasonable. Personal freedom has become a huge political issue, especially with regard to what people can and cannot do in their own home, to themselves and to each other.

Postmodernity is about the rise of diversity, choice and the end of rationality: the end of claims to absolute knowledge where truth becomes relative. All claims to truth are as true as each other. Therefore, medical science does not represent a better or the best way of controlling our bodies and our families. We cannot say that it is more truthful than the Protestant religious discourses that were used before modernity to control the body and limit sexuality within the family. All we can say is that, now, there are different choices. We now know that, since roughly the mid-1970s, aspects of family have changed in significant ways. The divorce rate was increasing at this time and continued to rise for the next 15 years, leading to the creation of a different range of 'partnership formations' (Allan 2009). The age of marriage, for example, began to increase, as did cohabitation; more people remained unmarried and women had fewer children. Essentially, what had been a close relationship between sex, marriage and childbirth became much less so. Furthermore, the 'construction' of families has become much more fluid and changeable. A common pattern of family has become much less likely, with many people experiencing reconstituted, blended families during their life course. Gay partnerships are now more accepted and, since the change in the law that allowed civil partnerships, gay couples can have a legal 'marriage' that gives them the same rights as heterosexual couples. The diversity in patterns of cohabitation, marriage, having and rearing children, separation, re-partnering, divorce, and lone parenthood are all aspects of the new 'family realm' (Allan 2009). However, within the sociology of the family there is an assumption that tends to underpin research and interest in topics about the family, this is termed 'hetero-normativity' – the assumption that all people are or should be heterosexual and that those who are not are deviant. For some postmodernists, this variety and diversity means liberation: choices can be made by the individual about how to get through life – choices about family, sexuality, partnership, raising children and what we do with our own bodies.

Although for Foucault the family is characterized by the dark side of life, postmodernists are a little more optimistic about family choice.

The strengths and weaknesses of the postmodern image of family choice and liberation

Strengths of Morgan's postmodern argument

- the postmodern perspective allows for individual free will within the family, rather than seeing individuals as nothing more than puppets of the family
- families are treated as different and unique – not generalizable
- the postmodern perspective sees families as living, growing and changing over time – not as fixed, static entities.

Weaknesses of Morgan's postmodern argument

- family diversity is not necessarily the same as liberation and choice: we cannot assume – as many postmodernists do – that the fragmentation of a single dominant family structure will lead to liberation. It may, instead, lead to even more ways in which families exercise control over those within them.
- feminists and Marxists argue that postmodern ideas on the family – since they concentrate on action within family relationships – virtually ignore the fact that families are shaped by the overarching nature of society and, therefore, benefit those who themselves benefit from the way in which society is structured: in other words, postmodernists ignore both capitalist and patriarchical influences on the family.

Ⓘ Ⓐ Ⓔ

Exercise 5.8

'Postmodernity is about the rise of diversity, choice and the end of rationality.' In order to investigate the extent to which this statement is true for family life, it would be useful to work as a group. A number of writers have shown how many more choices are available to us today than in the recent past. There is far more variety in both family structures and relationships.

For the individual, there are frequent choices to be made at every stage of life, and many of these choices were not faced by our grandparents, or even our parents. For example, if in the 1950s a teenage girl became pregnant, this probably caused considerable gossip and scandal, and shame for her family. She would probably have been pressed to marry the father, or have the child adopted. Today, with changed attitudes towards what is considered as acceptable social behaviour, a young woman in these circumstances is likely either to have an abortion or to keep the child, becoming a single-parent family. Indeed, the number of teenagers in this last category has risen considerably in recent years.

This is just one example – we could find similar cases for contraception, marriage, childbirth, divorce and so on. Your task is to do just that. As a group, you should work through the stages of a person's life and think about the decisions involved at each stage. Work out how many options are open to that person at each point. You should also try to find out what options were available in the past. You could ask your parents, grandparents or friends for any examples they can remember. Enter your findings in an extended version of the table below. One example is provided as an illustration of what is required.

Stage of life and situation	Options available in the past	Additional options available today
Teenager 1. Unplanned pregnancy	(a) Marriage (b) Adoption	(a) Bringing up child alone (b) Abortion

Ⓚ Ⓘ Ⓐ

Exercise 5.9

Read Item B, and answer the following questions:

1. Why are many cases of wife-battering not reported to the police?
2. In what ways are men able to dominate their wives? (Do not limit your answer to physical domination.)
3. What do Dobash and Dobash suggest are the main reasons why some men beat their wives? Try to identify several immediate causes, or 'triggers', plus some causes arising from the attitudes and inequalities found in the wider society.
4. Why do many women fail to leave their violent husbands? (Several reasons are mentioned in Item B, but you should be able to think of several more.)
5. Why are the police often reluctant to get involved with cases of domestic violence?

You will find some ideas for your answers in the passage from Item B, but you will need to build on these ideas by discussing the issue with other students.

Pahl (1980) notes that male physical violence against women in the home is often coupled with male control of economic power: many battered wives are kept in an acute state of poverty by their husbands – forcing them to stay in the marriage, rather than run away and seek help and refuge. Thus, we have here both economic patriarchy and physical patriarchy in the home.

Abbott and Wallace (1997) have identified three main explanations for male violence against women:

- *The traditionalist account*. According to this view, male violence is infrequent and, whilst not all female victims are responsible for the male violence against them, many incite attention that results in male sexual excitement. This view has caused great outrage among feminists and other schools of thought.
- *The liberal/psychiatric account*. According to this view, male violence is rare, but when it does occur it is a serious problem, and one that is caused by 'sick' or 'ill' individuals. This view is frequently favoured by the mass media.
- *The feminist account*. The feminist account of male violence starts by pointing out that the other two accounts are 'malestream' – they lack a genuine understanding of the lives of women and, in some cases, either ignore the issue, or actually attempt to blame women for the violence inflicted on them.

Although there are many different feminist views on male violence, feminists are united in their belief that male violence is rooted in patriarchal social relations.

For radical feminist Susan Brownmiller (1976), rape is a patriarchal act and 'natural' to the biological drive of all men. Rape is seen as a mechanism of control that is exercised by all men over all women. Rape is the same thing as male biological sexuality and it is an ever-present feature in all societies dominated by men.

Lynne Segal (1987) agrees with Brownmiller that rape acts as a form of social control, but she sees the act of rape as political rather than biological: It causes women to live their lives in fear, both in the home and outside in more public spheres of life.

For many women, sexual assault in the home is combined with physical assault that is not necessarily sexual in nature. For example, Sassetti (1993) estimates that in the United States between two and four million women are battered each year by their husbands. Some put this figure even higher at eight million.

According to Cheal (1991), domestic violence remains hidden in the private and isolated family because many agencies – state or otherwise – are still not fully prepared to become involved in the day-to-day lives of private families. This is due to three interrelated assumptions about family life contained within the familiar ideology held by the state (and supported by many on the New Right):

- *Access*: since the family is private, access by state agencies should be limited
- *Agency*: individuals are free social actors; therefore, if a woman is experiencing abuse, she is free to leave and/or seek help – this is not always the case, as demonstrated by Pahl (1980)
- *Interest*: the family is good for society and, therefore, we should protect the continuation of the family – it is in everyone's greater interests.

CHILD ABUSE

According to official figures, in the UK between one and two children per week die of neglect and/or abuse, half (52 per cent) of which incidents are caused by a parent. Cruelty towards and neglect of children has probably been an historical feature of many societies, and our increased awareness of it more to do with an increase in the reporting of it. However, in recent years the media has focused on some particularly abhorrent cases, and there have been changes in the law as a consequence of these. Probably one of the most influential cases was that of Victoria Climbié who died aged eight at the hands of her guardian, her great-aunt, in 2000. As a result of her death, a public inquiry was set up, which resulted in the creation of the policy initiative 'Every Child Matters'. Although there was evidence from several reports from Victoria's school, Church, social services and the police of signs of abuse, there was deemed to have been 'blinding incompetence' on the part of the authorities to investigate these reports and take action. The lack of communication between the various agencies who were dealing with her case was highlighted as an important factor in her death. The Every Child Matters initiative was supposed to streamline children's services so that, when a child was suspected of being at risk, a multi-agency approach was adopted that would ensure that a lead professional coordinated the action deemed necessary in the case. Child protection and safeguarding were supposed to be the top government and local authority priorities. However, another child – this time much younger, at eighteen months old – was killed at the hands of his mother, her boyfriend and their lodger in 2007. Baby P (Peter Connolly) died of over 50 physical injuries, including a broken back and broken ribs in August 2007, despite being seen by numerous doctors and social workers throughout his short life. The resulting inquiry into Baby P's death called Haringay Social Services and Great Ormond Street hospital to account for failing to detect his injuries and prevent his harrowing death. The director of social services was sacked by the then Minister Ed Balls and the hospital's child development completely re-organized.

Exam focus

1. How might feminist sociologists explain domestic violence and account for the power of men in families?
2. Our views of childhood have changed over time and vary between societies. How might these different views of childhood influence the ways children are treated?
3. How far does the functionalist perspective describe the family? What evidence is there that would refute the image painted by the functionalists?

Important concepts

Ideology • Surveillance • Moral panic • Dysfunction • Domestic violence • Child abuse • Forced marriage • Honour killing

Critical thinking

1. Is the evidence of the negative side of family life – child abuse, domestic violence, high divorce rate – sufficient for us to argue that the family is no longer an institution to be valued in society?
2. How far is it the case that women and children are the unlucky victims of power struggles within the family?
3. Why is it still the case that the police and courts fails to adequately deal with violence in the family, as evidenced by the numbers of women killed annually by their partners and the low incidence of conviction for rape?

Chapter 6

The Impact of Industrialization: Changes in Family Structure

By the end of this chapter you should:

- be able to explain the transition from pre-industrial to industrial society and its effects on the family
- be familiar with conflicting evidence on the changing family
- appreciate the arguments for and against the existence of the 'symmetrical family'
- understand the importance of historical evidence
- be familiar with recent studies of family structure
- be familiar with the differences between modern and post-modern family structures
- be able to apply ideas of the family and its relationship to industrialization to assessment requirements

INTRODUCTION

It takes only a little imagination to realize that the major social change that occurred in many societies – the movement from a predominantly rural society and economy to one that was mainly urban and industrial – inevitably brought with it drastic and far-reaching adaptations in the daily lives of the population. These changes affected people's relationships, their life-patterns and thinking. From an agricultural society where most of the population lived and worked on the land – a society of little movement, low technology and limited means of communication – there was a move towards an industrial and late-industrial society of tremendous variety.

Today, we have mass communication and travel, continual movement and adaptation in social, geographical and economic terms. In addition, in more recent years postmodernist thinkers – such as the geographer David Harvey (1989) – have pointed to the process

Item A

- According to Laslett (1965), the average household size was 4.75 persons during the pre-industrial period.
- Most people (53 per cent) lived in households containing six or more people.
- Important factors mentioned by Laslett include:
  - low life-expectancy
  - late marriage
  - late childbirth
  - large numbers of children
  - servants working in families.

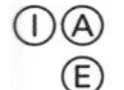

Exercise 6.2

Study Item A and answer the following questions:

1. 'What existed in pre-industrial times were probably nuclear families in large households.' Explain how each of the points listed in Item A contributes to a justification of this statement.
2. Is household size likely to be a very accurate measure of family size? Take into account each of the following:
   - some households contain only one person;
   - there are a variety of family structures;
   - extended families might live in several different households but still act as a single family.

Historical evidence 2: the family and modernity

Anderson – the sociology of the family Michael Anderson's (1971) study of the nineteenth-century family structure, based on census data for Preston in 1851, presents an image of the early industrial family that is very much in line with that described by Starkey. The picture is one of strengthening and broadening kinship ties in a growing industrial town. Anderson asserts that the process of industrialization, and its affects on migration and the pattern of daily life, led to a greater need amongst the new working classes for family support and solidarity. Rather than encouraging a nuclear family structure, therefore, the percentage of households that contained kin from outside the nuclear family rose to 23 per cent, higher than in both pre-industrial Britain and modern industrial Britain. No longer self-reliant in terms of food production and shelter, subject to the vagaries of the industrial economy and without any help from a state welfare system, family members turned to each other for support. The extended family seems to have acted as a sort of mutual aid organization, providing insurance against unemployment, sickness and old age. Both in times of crisis and in everyday life, families could help. Older relatives could provide child care for mothers – in return, receiving support and care themselves in old age. Orphans and other young family members might be taken in by relatives to become working lodgers and add to the total family income. Liz Stanley (1992), when studying Rochdale in the 1980s, looked back to the town in the 1880s and found a similar situation to that described by Anderson. In particular, she shows the way in which the 1980s mirrored the 1880s with regard to the relatively high rate of female employment, and the complexity of families and households – a similarity that she attributes to the lack of regulation in the labour market during both these decades.

Item B

The mid- and late-Victorian economy, particularly in areas where textiles were important, was subject to sharp cyclical patterns of downturn and upturn. In a social and political context where there were no state benefits designed to help people cope with economic misfortune, there were a variety of strategies that people utilized to manage as best they could in such circumstances.

Seasonal opportunities in agriculture were still widely available until approximately the end of the century; and the emptying out of factories and workshops at certain key periods in the agricultural year was noted by many contemporary commentators.

The Victorian economy, even in areas dominated by particular kinds of employment, as parts of the Northwest were dominated by textile manufacture, was still a very mixed one; and a large informal economy existed in complex relationship with the formal economy, in which people participated in increased numbers in periods of downturn in the formal economy. Both economies were characterized by insecurity of employment, bad working conditions, low pay, casualisation of labour, labour externalization in the form of homeworking and workshop-based production.

For many people, particularly but not exclusively women, domestic service acted as employment of last resort. However, often 'domestic service' in census data was in fact a gloss on something more complex. Sometimes non-employed relatives living in a household were recorded as domestic servants, presumably because they serviced other employed members of the household in return for board and lodging. Also, other people worked as domestic servants outside of the households in which they were living, but for other family members, suggesting that the key factor here might be family/household support to people without other gainful employment.

The majority of women, certainly the large majority of those employed in the skilled and well-paid textile jobs, worked full-time throughout the life-course; and often their employment was more skilled, better paid and more secure than that of male partners.

This employment status of women had all kinds of consequences; one which was often noted by middle-class contemporaries was the 'cheek' of women textile workers, their failure to 'know their place', their loudness and 'unladylike' behaviour in public places (and from which was drawn usually erroneous conclusions about their sexual 'immorality'). Another was their high levels of unionization, political radicalism and political activism in a variety of radical causes.

letters and so on – enabled families to keep in close contact, even when living in different parts of the country. Litwak coined the term 'modified extended family' to describe this situation, emphasizing the connections between families, rather than their isolation.

Similar evidence emerged in Britain in subsequent years. In the 1960s, a study was carried out by Rosser and Harris (1965) of working-class families in Swansea. They, too, found that the entirely isolated nuclear family was a rare occurrence. In this case, strong sentimental ties had replaced the family cohesion brought about by practical help for each other. Improvements in educational provision and the diversification of employment had made the family less close-knit, but the extended family was still strong in its ties of affection. The two main functions fulfilled by extended kin ties were social identity and social support, particularly in times of crisis, when relatives were the first port of call for help. Rosser and Harris also noted that the greater the level of female domesticity in the family, the stronger the degree of family cohesion. Research by Charles *et al.* (2008) updated the Rosser and Harris (1965) study of the family in Swansea by carrying out a survey of 1000 households and conducting ethnographic interviewing. They found that the time spent living in a nuclear-family household is now much shorter for the majority of younger people (under 50). Also, a significant number of couples now have no children and the proportion of the population who were single had increased from 11.8 per cent to 19.9 per cent. Charles *et al.* also found that the extended family consisting of three generations living under one roof had declined from 1 in 5 households in 1960 to 1 in 200 in 2002, the only section of the population where three generation families remain is the Bangladeshi community, which forms the largest minority ethnic group in Swansea. Where mothers and daughters led similar daily lives, family cohesion was very strong, especially when the daughter was married. In the updated research, Charles *et al.* also found that, with the increase in women working, the proportion of mothers and partnered daughters having daily contact had fallen, but mothers and daughters had the most contact of all individuals. However, the ethnographic research also found that close networks of family and friends were still evident, especially in the working-class neighbourhoods and amongst the minority ethnic population. Colin Bell (1968) found a similar picture amongst middle-class families in the same town. Again, the family was a source of aid and service in times of difficulty or crisis. Greater geographical distances meant little day-to-day contact, but longer visits and telephone calls maintained a close relationship – mostly with grandparents, but also with other kin: neighbours had not significantly replaced these ties. A particular family service found by Bell was the support (financial and social) provided for young middle-class couples in the initial home-making and child-rearing stages of their life – a time when they would find it difficult to maintain their middle-class lifestyle alone. The bond between father and son or son-in-law meant that substantial aid was given by the senior couple to the junior – presents for the home that were out of proportion to the occasion, large gifts of toys to the children. Bell suggested that all of these served as 'status props' for the young family, helping to maintain and improve their status.

In research conducted in the late 1980s by Peter Willmott in a suburb of North London, there was evidence that contact with kin remained an important aspect of family life for both the middle and working classes . Even when families lived some distance from their in-laws, they maintained regular weekly contact and the differences between the middle and working class were not really significant. Keeping in touch by telephone was maintained, if the distance to visit was too great. In the 2000s, we could assume that email, Facebook and Skype would also be used as a means of keeping in contact with our 'dispersed' families.

Ⓐ **Exercise 6.6**

Carry out a quick survey of your friends to find out who keeps in touch with their distant relatives via an electronic medium – videophone, text, email, social networking sites and so on. What can this tell us about the changing ways in which we relate to each other?

THE SYMMETRICAL FAMILY

In the 1970s, the debates on the nature of the modern family became more complex. Much of the discussion initially centred on a further study by Young and Willmott (1975) in London, 20 years after their Bethnal Green study. This study was called *The Symmetrical Family*. Young and Willmott outlined the three stages through which they believed the family had progressed, with a further stage predicted for the future.

Stage 1: the pre-industrial family

In this period, the family was a unit of production, the members working together, mostly in agriculture. Examples of this stage can still be found today in farming areas.

Stage 2: the early industrial family

This was the family of the industrial revolution, 'torn apart' by the economic and social changes. It characteristically had extended kinship networks to provide support and aid in times of need. There were mother–daughter ties that held the family together, but often only a weak relationship between husband and wife – they tended to have separate roles, carrying out their own chores and responsibilities. Examples of this stage can also be found in Anderson (1971) and Young and Willmott (1962).

Stage 3: the symmetrical family

This is the modern nuclear family of today. According to Young and Willmott, it has three main characteristics:

- *This family is predominantly nuclear, not extended.* The nuclear family is much more isolated from extended kin, and members depend far more on each other for help and companionship.
- *Life in the modern family is home-centred* – the home itself is much more comfortable and family life is more affluent, so the home has become a pleasant place for the whole family to spend their leisure time.

- Many feminists have attacked the idea of the .... with 'joint conjugal roles'. Ann Oakley (1974a) considers that this argument is based on very flimsy evidence.
- Feminists also argue that the roles of husbands and wives are still very ...., most chores still being done by wives with only a little help from their husbands.
- There is little evidence of the process of stratified diffusion, or that it has led to a stage 4 family. The growth in the proportion of .... makes this unlikely.
- As part of the 'march of progress', Young and Willmott have been criticized for their neglect of the possible .... of the modern family.

Missing words

- symmetrical family
- working married women
- unequal
- negative and conflict aspects
- extended family
- women

OTHER STUDIES OF FAMILY STRUCTURE

In the late 1980s and 1990s, researchers returned to the question of the isolation and 'privatization' of the nuclear family. Fiona Devine (1992) revisited the subject matter of Goldthorpe and Lockwood's research in Luton in the 1960s (Goldthorpe *et al.* 1969). During their study of affluent car workers at the Vauxhall plant in Luton, Goldthorpe and Lockwood had found a high level of privatization amongst working-class families – their home-centred existence appeared to have isolated them from extended kin and other working-class families. In contrast, the families studied by Devine in the late 1980s had regular contacts with kin. This contact was particularly strong between grandparents, parents and children. Although families were often geographically isolated, just as the studies by Bell, Litwak and others found in the 1960s, Devine discovered that distance was not necessarily an impediment to regular contact – cars and telephones were frequently used.

The work of Janet Finch (1989) has centred largely on family obligations – how these might have altered as a consequence of social change, and the extent to which the sense of obligation still exists. To what extent, in both the past and the present, have relatives felt obliged to give each other support, whether practical, financial or social?

It is often assumed that a pre-industrial '*golden age*' once existed, when family obligations were clear and adherence to them was widespread. Finch (1989) argues against the notion of a 'golden age' of relatives helping and assuming responsibility for each other as an automatic duty. In a time when life expectancy was lower, there were certainly fewer elderly people to be looked after. The principle of primogeniture (the passing on of the family estate to the first-born only) meant that parents did not normally make provision for their other children. Where kin did provide aid or live together in the same household, it was usually out of mutual self-interest or to keep down household expenditure.

Research in the 2000s by Finch (2007) introduced another concept – 'display' – to add to the sociological 'tool kit' when trying to understand contemporary family relationships. She argues that the concept of 'display' helps us to understand more clearly what families *do*, rather than focusing on the traditional 'structures' to which individuals belong. The emphasis is on how people create their own understanding of what their 'family' is and what their family relationships mean. The social nature of family practices is at the heart of this way of viewing the family because there can be many different interpretations of actions that constitute 'family practices'. Hence, for Finch, display 'is a process by which individuals, and groups of individuals, convey to each other and to relevant audiences that certain of their actions do constitute "doing family things" and thereby confirm that these relationships are "family" relationships' (2009: 72).

Valentine *et al.* (2003) argue that the reworking of traditional hierarchies and expectations within family life has led to a weakening of constraints and social norms as applied to individuals. Hence, individuals are free to choose a variety of options in relation to their pursuit of identity and happiness. Notably, they argue, this has led to more opportunities for lesbians and gay men to 'come out', and thereby negotiate their identities with others in their 'families' and beyond. The notion of individualization is important here and relates to the apparent freedom experienced by men and women to experiment with their identities, relationships, actions, reactions both within and beyond the family. Thus, 'doing' the family is increasingly the area of interest for sociologists. Research into these areas is becoming known as a field in its own right and is referred to as the 'sociology of emotions' (Valentine 2003).

Evidence from empirical studies (Weeks *et al.* 2001, Williams 2004, Office for National Statistics 2008) suggests that, because of changing patterns of living, it is increasingly difficult for people to define a family structure. Diversity in the ways families are composed over time due to divorce, re-partnering and the creation of stepfamilies, changes in patterns of living and 'fluidity' in family relationships are all evidence of the difficulty of stating what constitutes a family. According to official figures in the UK, the traditional nuclear family containing a heterosexual couple and their dependent children constituted less than one fifth of households in 2007. Between 1971 and 2007, the largest decline in households was in this 'traditional household' (*Social Trends* 2008). By contrast, the proportion of households containing one individual has more than doubled (*Social Trends* 2008). There has also been a marked increase in the proportion of people cohabiting and a trend towards later marriage.

These recent changes in family structure and form bring into question the impact of major societal changes – such as industrialization – on the family. Since the nineteenth century, there have been many other changes – such as technological innovation, the introduction of the car and air travel, changes in working practices and what is produced, globalization and women working, to name a few. It would be extremely difficult to isolate each of these factors to explain changes in the family. We now must take into account factors such as ethnicity, individualization and questions of gender identity, when we consider the nature and extent of family ties and obligations. Finch and Mason's (1993) study of the family in Greater Manchester found that actual help given to family members – such as financial, emotional, practical and child care –was still widespread. More recently, we seem to have broadened our networks to include friends.

with so many choices and so many possibilities, it is impossible to tell right from wrong, true from false – or even the real from the unreal. There are no overarching, dominant claims to truth – claims of universal knowledge – that we can use to make sense of the world.

One key feature of the rise of this postmodern relativism is that human actors have become increasingly aware of this situation and of the need to deal with this plurality, this fragmentation of reality. Individuals have become freer to choose lifestyles that will give meaning to their life. What this means in terms of changes to the family is that we can no longer point to a single, all-encompassing family type or structure and say, with certainty, that this type of family is the most common or, indeed, as – functionalists and the New Right claim – that this type of family is somehow better than another. Whereas the traditional/premodern and modern stages of historical social development can be seen as characterized by a universal family structure, this is not the case, today. We are now faced with family diversity, as discussed in Chapter 8.

Item D

Table 6.2 Households by size, Great Britain, 1971–2008 (%)

	1971	1981	1991	2001	2008
1 person	18	22	27	29	29
2 people	32	32	34	35	35
3 people	19	17	16	16	16
4 people	17	18	16	14	13
5 people	8	7	5	5	5
6 or more people	6	4	2	2	2
All households (= 100%) (millions)	18.6	20.2	22.4	23.9	25.0
Average household size (number of people)	2.9	2.7	2.5	2.4	2.4

Source: Census, Labour Force Survey, Office for National Statistics.

ⒾⒶ

Exercise 6.13

Study Item D and answer the following questions:

1. Between 1971 and 2008, the largest increase occurred in the number of people living alone. Who do you think these people are? Name three groups of people who are most likely to live alone. What are their age groups likely to be? What gender? What social and economic circumstances are they likely to be in?

2. Apart from one-person households, which is the only other category that increased in proportion over this period?
3. Which categories decreased the most? Think of three possible reasons for this decline.
4. Write a short paragraph to explain the main trends over time displayed in Item D. It helps to look at the main axis first to make sure you have understood the key points such as the years represented, percentages and so on.

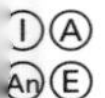

Exercise 6.14

A wide range of theories and research has looked at the impact of industrialization on the family. The discussion is still continuing today and research on the state of the family in the 2000s is being added to the existing body of knowledge. This area of research has also led to and/or been influenced by other areas in the study of the family.

We saw in Chapter 3 how functionalist writers such as Talcott and Parsons based many of their theories of the modern family on the assumption that there had been a transition from the pre-industrial extended family to the modern nuclear family in industrial society. The conflicting evidence discussed in this chapter clearly leads us to question this in many ways.

1. Find some examples in this chapter that question the traditional functionalist perspective on the 'theory of transition'.
2. Much of the work that questions the changing roles of men and women has come from feminists. For example, we have seen in this present chapter and in Chapter 4 how feminist sociologists show how the coming of later industrial society affected the position of women, both at work and in the home, leading to the emergence of a 'female' domestic sphere and making women from all classes more dependent on men. Feminists have also mounted the most critical attacks on the notion of the 'symmetrical family' and whether Young and Willmott (1975) were really talking about conjugal equality.

   'What Young and Willmott took for symmetry in the 1970s, we would take to be inequality today.' Explain what this statement means in terms of changing attitudes and expectations.
3. Chapter 7, on roles and relationships, looks more closely at how relationships between husbands and wives seem to have changed and what aspects of them seem to have remained much the same over time. You will find that much of the research discussed puts into question the whole idea of a predominant symmetrical family in modern Britain.

   What sorts of activities and responsibilities in the home would you need to investigate in order to prove whether or not couples had 'joint conjugal roles'? Jot these down and compare them later with the research discussed in Chapter 7.
4. Chapter 8 considers the growing diversity of family and household structures, suggesting that there is certainly not one typical modern family structure, but that a wide variety of household compositions and relationships exist side by side in modern society. Postmodernists assert that concepts such as 'the symmetrical family' are not useful because they classify into false categories situations that are both fluid and complex.

Critical thinking

1. In what ways can we define 'the family'?
2. Is it sufficient to link changes in the family to an economic/industrial process? What other factors have effected changes in the family?
3. Are we moving to a new kind of postmodern family? If so, what are its key features?

Chapter 7

Family Roles, Marriage and Relationships

By the end of this chapter you should:

- have an understanding of family roles and their importance for self-identity from an interpretive perspective
- be able to apply an interpretive perspective to the study of the family
- be aware of the strengths and weaknesses of the interpretive approach
- understand the differences between structural and action approaches to the study of the family
- have knowledge and sociological understanding of sex, sexuality and 'romantic love'
- have knowledge of 'conjugal roles' and parenthood, and be able to apply a feminist perspective to the study of these roles
- be able to apply modernist and postmodernist perspectives to family sociology
- be able to apply the ideas of risk society and reflexive modernization to the study of the family
- be able to apply these ideas to assessment requirements

INTRODUCTION

In Chapter 5, we discussed the functions and dysfunctions (the 'dark side') of family life, but we have yet to investigate in detail the patterns of day-to-day, 'ordinary' life in families. To do this, we need to employ sociological perspectives that operate on more micro (small-scale) levels, rather than the structural or systems approaches (see Chapter 3), as exemplified by Marxism and feminism.

The value of the interpretive or phenomenological approaches is precisely that they offer an alternative to structural views. They allow us to concentrate on individual action and interaction, and investigate what being in a family means to those involved: a technique referred to as '*verstehen*' by many phenomenologists, meaning 'to see the world through the eyes of those involved'.

a partner, that cultures of intimacy and care centre on friendship groupings and have moved beyond the 'heteronormative' family. Roseneil and Budgeon have focused on two themes: the importance of friendship within everyday life taking over from family relationships, and the 'decentring' of conjugal relationships, which reconfigures domestic space and challenges the nuclear family structure. Essentially, this means that there is a range of other domestic and family relationships that are becoming as important, if not more important, than the traditional conjugal relationship. The research has also pointed to the fluidity between notions of friends – sometimes connected with work, and lovers, as well as their interchangeability over time. However, this research is based a small number of case studies and cannot be said to be representative of a wider population. Nonetheless, this is an example of the ways in which sociologists are now adopting an interpretive perspective to try to understand how individuals are making sense of their identities and family roles in modern times, when the notion of a family structure is much more contested.

Ⓐ

Exercise 7.2

You may have noticed that, when visiting another family, some patterns of behaviour, customs or traditions in that family are rather different from your own. Some things may seem very unfamiliar but, in the same way, many taken-for-granted aspects of your own family life may seem rather strange to others.

As a group, find as many examples of this as you can. Compare notes about family habits:

- Who does what?
- How are things organized?
- Are there any unwritten rules that are implicitly understood but not voiced?
- What expectations are understood?
- Consider a number of areas of everyday life, such as eating, chores, visiting, washing and so on.

You may find some that are very amusing to outsiders!

What are relationships in the family really like?

This is the central question posed by interpretive sociologists when looking at the family. They ask, what is family life really like for those who are involved in its active creation? What roles are required to be performed in the home? What scripts are available for us to follow? We shall look here at three examples of interpretive studies on the family before turning our attention to specific issues and themes of relationships in the family.

Berger and Kellner (1980 [1964]) look at socially constructed roles in a marriage: what does it mean to take on – or, rather, to act out – the role of husband or wife? How does one play the role of a married person, and how does one learn the script of this role? They argue that, as with any other reality, the reality of a marriage is an ongoing construction: it has to be constantly reaffirmed, negotiated and renegotiated. All human meaning and action is seen as being fragile in this way.

Mansfield and Collard (1988) adopt an interpretive position when studying the processes that take place between making the decision to marry and actually becoming married. As Berger and Kellner (1980 [1964]), Mansfield and Collard are interested in how the shared meaning of marriage is a product of negotiation between those involved in its active creation. Newly-married partners have to renegotiate aspects of their lives that they previously took for granted – for example, the spending of wages, domestic tasks and so on.

David Clark (1991), also using the interpretive approach, has conducted a study of how couples construct a meaningful marriage in the first few months of their married relationship. Clark used the methodological technique of the in-depth interview, which is ideally suited to uncovering the meanings and motives of social reality.

Clark seeks to further the understanding of the often private, closed and intimate world of marriage. How does marriage make sense to those 'doing marriage'? As with all types of face-to-face, day-to-day interaction, marriage is seen as an active process. It is something we 'do', something individuals 'make' together.

Clark identifies four types of marriage. This identification of types of interaction as a methodological technique has its origins in the work of Max Weber – the founder of the interpretive or phenomenological approach discussed here. According to Weber, sociologists can construct what he called 'ideal-types' of society: lists of features or ingredients that can be 'matched' or compared with social reality in order to understand what individuals actually do. Clark argues that there are:

- '*drifting marriages*': where meanings and ideas about the future of the new family are unclear.
- '*surfacing marriages*': these are often made up of people who have been married before – what we call a 'reconstituted family' – and there is often concern about the intrusion of previous relationships into the new one
- '*establishing marriages*': here the newly-wed couple plan and try to negotiate a long-term future reality
- '*struggling marriages*': marriages with financial problems – often due to unemployment; these problems cause tension and anxiety in the relationship.

Ⓘ Ⓐ Ⓐⁿ Ⓔ

Exercise 7.3

Each marriage develops in its own way as an active process. We often hear that marriage has to be 'worked at'; it does not start off as a finished product. A couple may need to negotiate many aspects of daily life. In doing so, they arrive at a shared meaning of marriage, though this shared meaning can change constantly and may break down completely.

What must be negotiated? The list can be almost endless. In a table copied from the one below, try to put together a list of what may need to be negotiated as a marriage begins and develops – this could range from a negotiated decision about what tea to use or how many tea bags, to something as major as whether or when to have children. We have provided some examples to start you off.

Area of life	Examples of issues to be negotiated
Money	Who pays the bills? Who buys the groceries? Joint bank account or separate? Regular savings? By whom? How much personal spending?
Chores	
Sex	
Relationships with relatives	
Discipline of children	
Responsibility for children	
Going out	
Holidays	

Ⓐ Ⓐⓝ Ⓔ

Exercise 7.4

Write an account using a feminist approach of the process of negotiation. What would a feminist sociologist see as the importance of patriarchy in this process?

More recent approaches that have also been influenced by a micro-sociology perspective

Research conducted by Carrington (1999) does not approach the family as an institution, or through the kinship connections associated with the conventional family; instead, he sees the family as a series of activities, or how people 'do' the family. In his study of gay and lesbian households in California, he tries to understand how family is achieved through the various different kinds of work undertaken in the family – what he calls *kin work*, *feeding work*, *consumption work*, *care work*.

Finch (2007) has developed the notion of 'display' to illustrate and help to understand the changed social environment in which family life now takes place. All empirical research and statistical evidence points to the diversity of family composition and the fluidity of family relationships. The people who we see as our family will change over time and during our life course. Many groups are unable to point to a static domestic arrangement that they call a family – these groups include those who choose who they live with, same-sex partnerships, friendship groups, children, and adults who are divorced. Individuals may be part of different households – such as stepchildren, step-parents, those who are co-parenting, those born as a result of reproductive technologies, those with transnational kin relationships, to name a few.

Finch (2007) goes on to argue that there are three dimensions to display that need to be considered, given the nature of the changing social context within which 'family' takes place. First, that the family does not equate to household – by this, Finch is pointing to the fact that the household in which one *currently* lives will not necessarily remain the same over time. Households will change with divorce, re-partnering, the addition of children/stepchildren, separation and/or death, so that during a life course we may experience a nuclear family, single-parent family, blended family, single person status and, perhaps, several of these. Second, Finch discusses the fluidity of families over time. She points out that, although families have always changed over time, there is an increasing volatility in contemporary families. This leads to the need for relationships to be defined, redefined, and established and re-established, and this is done through the overt family practices and display. For example, after divorce, a reconstituted family may make clear that stepchildren have a place in the new family and are fully involved in all family activities. So, a process of readjustment takes place whereby individuals redefine their identities in the evolutionary process of recreating a family. The third way in which display is important is linked to the personal identity of "non-heterosexuals" (Weeks *et al.* 2001), who choose a family structure to underpin their lifestyle. The blurring of kinship, friendship and intimate relationships suggests that the choosing of family relationships is widespread (Finch and Mason 1993, Plummer 1995, Morgan 1996, Weeks *et al.* 2001). These chosen 'families' that support intimate relationships involve a complex interplay between social processes, personal intimacy and personal identity. They are a means by which new types of relationships can be forged and used to reinforce a life style –'doing' family but in a new context, trying to establish a different family but seeking legitimacy, too. This can apply to heterosexual families as well as homosexual families.

Finch uses the term 'display' not only as a way to describe how family actions and activities denote that the group are a family, and thereby are given meaning by participants, but also as an analytical tool that sociologists can use to try to understand the reconfiguration of 'family' and family relationships in contemporary society – 'doing family things, not 'being' a family'.

Strengths and weaknesses of interpretive sociology

The value – or main strength – of the interpretive approach, in general, is that it allows us to uncover and to understand meanings: to 'get into the heads' of those in society and to study culture as made up of thoughts, feelings and emotions. In contrast, more structural and positivistic sociologists ignore thoughts and feelings because they believe that these cannot be directly observed and, therefore, cannot be studied in a 'scientific' fashion. In terms of the sociology of the family, the interpretive approach means that we can uncover the meanings and 'reality' of an otherwise 'private' area of society.

On the other hand, the main weakness of the interpretive approach is that it often ignores the fact that our private and emotional lives are shaped by wider structural forces.

Strengths

- Unlike more macro perspectives such as Marxism and functionalism, the interpretive approach studies how individuals make families through their interactions with each other.
- Interpretive sociology is not interested in generalizations about family life, but seeks to understand how families are both a usual aspect of reality, and yet unique and individualistic.

- Interpretive sociology explores the differences between the common-sense image of family life we all have, and what the meanings of 'families' actually are in society. This is very different from functionalism, which often takes the common sense of the family at face value.
- Interpretive ideas on, and methods of, studying the family are often taken up by other theories and used to supplement their macro theorizing.

Weaknesses

- While concentrating on meanings, motives and action, it ignores the wider structures in which families operate and are shaped.
- Although families are unique, sometimes generalizations are useful as they allow politicians to consider social policies towards the family: interpretive sociology cannot contribute easily to debates on broader policy as it is too individualistic.

The problem of the separation of structure from action was taken up by Anthony Giddens (1984) and has led to the creation of 'structurational sociology': the attempt to unite analysis of structure and action (agency) as one. This idea will be discussed in more detail at the end of this chapter.

SEX, SEXUALITY AND MARRIAGE: THE RISE OF ROMANTIC LOVE?

Having looked at interpretive ideas on the construction of families in day-to-day life, we shall now turn our attention to the idea of marriage and its relationships. We shall begin by considering some historical work on the rise of romance in married relationships, the nature of domestic labour and conjugal roles from a more feminist perspective; and then go on to discuss ideas of ideology and, eventually, modernity and postmodernity.

In his classic text *The Family, Sex and Marriage in England 1500–1800*, Lawrence Stone (1977) argues that the history of family structure and its internal relationships can be classified into three distinctive phases or types of family and marriage:

- the *open lineage family* (dominant by the sixteenth century in England). Here, the family and marriage were based not upon notions of love, but upon perceived obligations to other kin and the community. Marriages were not so much a union of partners as alliances between families.
- the *restricted patriarchal nuclear family* (the sixteenth to the eighteenth century). Here, the family and marriage became the concern of, and was strengthened by, the patriarchal nature of the state. The male head of household was given a position of strength to dominate children and women. This family type was only a temporary phase in the history of marriage, argues Stone, and was associated mainly with upper-class families and relationships.
- the *closed, domesticated nuclear family* (the basis of contemporary family life) is founded upon what Stone refers to as 'affective individualism': the belief that marriage should be based upon personal choice and freedom, as directed by notions of romantic love.

As can be seen, the idea that romantic love is the best basis for family life and marriage is a relatively recent cultural development, linked to the rise of individualism and the onset of industrialization and capitalism.

The family in the action–structure duality

The value of many of the contemporary ideas of writers such as Giddens is that they attempt to study both action and structure. For Giddens, this action–structure duality is a two-way street – we need to understand both. Giddens (1984) calls this 'structurational sociology' – the unification of the understanding of an individual agency and how this agency fits into wider patterns. On a macro level, society is seen as the ongoing construction of the individuals involved, but it is also a pattern that exists over time and is passed down the generations. It is especially useful when applied to an understanding of family relationships in the contemporary age. It allows us to use the insights of interpretive sociology along with other more structural perspectives – such as those of the various feminisms. It also provides a context for the critical evaluation of postmodern ideas.

Giddens has looked at how sexuality and intimacy are related to dominant discourses in society, and argues that sexuality is a social construction that has strong links to power relations between individuals and groups in society. He uses the term 'plastic sexuality' to describe the sexual revolution and use of reliable contraception, which has led to sex being freed from the reproductive process. Plastic sexuality can be moulded as a personality trait bound up with notions of identity and self. Giddens draws upon the work of Foucault to discuss how our attitudes, values and actions towards sex, intimacy and romantic love are related to aspects of identity and the general culture within a social order. A particular society and culture will give rise to the discourse about the nature of how these phenomena are thought about and understood. Attitudes are bound up with issues to do with self-discipline and the acceptability of roles and relationships between men and women. Gender, the ways in which we construct masculinity and femininity, is closely connected to the emergence of intimate, romantic relations between men and women. In different periods of history, the nature of these relationships changes; this confirms the socially constructed nature of these aspects of life that we often consider to be 'natural'. For example, in some societies marriage has been, and still is, seen as an economic relationship that can cement the ties between two families and provide economically for a number of different kin whereas, in other societies, marriage is based upon romantic love between a man and woman leading to individual fulfilment and satisfaction for them both.

We have seen how marriage based on the idea of romantic love is a relatively recent phenomenon. In the past, marriage was based much more on economic, practical and community considerations. Cross-cultural evidence shows us that such considerations are still very important in arranged marriages today. We tend to take for granted the type of relationship that is familiar and 'normal' to us, but we should also be able to see some of the advantages of alternative arrangements. For example, you may feel that parents are able to make a much more practical and lasting choice of partner for their offspring than young people can make for themselves (For more on arranged marriage, see Exercise 2.7, p. 000).

The view that romantic love as the basis of marriage and the family is a relatively recent social phenomenon is echoed by Philippe Ariès (1973). Ariès suggests that, before the rise

The symmetrical family?

For Young and Willmott (1975), roles within the family had become 'symmetrical' (see Chapters 4, 5 and 6). Husbands do their fair share of domestic chores compared with previously. This was seen by Young and Willmott as representing increased personal democracy in family life – a reflection of the increased personal democracy in society as a whole in the late industrial age. Evidence from other societies also suggested that conjugal roles had become more equal, regardless of culture or ethnicity. For example, Latino men in the United States, notwithstanding their reputation for machismo, had become more involved with the raising of their children and, despite outward appearances, it was Latina mothers who held power within the family setting (Brice 2002). Roopnarine and Gielen (2005), in reviewing global developments in conjugal roles, argued that there was a distinct, though not universal, shift towards less patriarchal forms of family engagement by men, but with resistance to major changes in male contributions also being a feature of the global trajectories of changes in household tasks.

Feminism and conjugal roles

In opposition to the claims made by Parsons, for Young and Willmott the study of conjugal roles links to feminist concerns about the unequal division of domestic labour in the home, as illustrated by the ideas of Gavron (1966) and Oakley on housework (1974a, 2005) (see Chapters 4 and 5). More recently, Coltrane (2000), in the United States, found that the average woman does twice as much housework as the average man. For many feminists, the unequal nature of conjugal roles leads to the 'captivity' of women in traditional gender roles: a feature of the dark side of the family from feminist and feminist-influenced viewpoints. This older research tended to use quantitative methods relying on the statistical results of interviews and the assumption of heteronormativity, (where heterosexuality is seen as the norm and other forms of sexual identity are defined as deviant). Subsequent research tends to be of a qualitative nature, using in-depth interviews and case studies that explore complex issues and perceptions of family life and roles connected to issues of identity, and conceptions of masculinity and femininity (Duncan 2006, Roseneil and Budgeon 2006, Finch 2007, Gatrell 2008). For example, in the case of care-giving, ideologically associated with the 'nurturing' nature of females, there is a host of evidence that it is women and girls who are predominately responsible for looking after children, the frail elderly, the disabled and the ill (see, e.g., Arendell 2000).

For Marxist-feminists, in particular, domestic labour epitomizes the nature of women's role in a capitalist society. Women produce the next generation of workers, servicing their needs and those of their husbands by carrying out the essential domestic tasks that enable them to be prepared for their working lives. Emotional as well as physical needs are met through the work of the housewife and mother, all free-of-charge for the capitalists.

Beck-Gernsheim (2002) has argued that the family becomes a transitional phase in people's lives – not disappearing altogether, but perhaps becoming a part-time commitment. However, despite that fact that married women are now in paid employment, gender stratification is still evident within families, with women continuing to outperform men in doing domestic labour. Even though the gap may be reduced, this is accounted for by women doing less housework as their time commitment to work outside the home increases.

An E

Exercise 7.6

When studying the evidence from various researchers on changes in conjugal roles, you may have reflected on the way things are organized in your own home. This exercise requires you to conduct a short quiz so that you can apply some of the relevant questions to your own experience.

Copy out and complete the table below, which lists the responsibilities likely to be found in most homes. Your first task is to decide who would have been assigned each responsibility in the past, in a situation of clearly segregated conjugal roles. When you have decided this, perhaps as a group, you then need individually to say who is now responsible in each case in your own home. Some of the examples may not apply to your home – for example, there may not be a baby or a small child, but you might be able to find out what happened when there was. Similarly, a responsibility may be taken by a son or daughter rather than a parent – in this case the important question to ask is, is it one specific gender?

Responsibility	Traditionally taken by	Taken in my home today by	Score
Washing up			
Replacing a fuse			
Ironing			
Mowing the lawn (or similar)			
Dusting			
Cooking family meals			
Climbing a ladder to an upper window			
Making beds			
Decorating			
Shopping for family groceries			
Unblocking the sink			
Family washing			
Looking after a sick child			
Bathing children/baby			

While ideological representations or discourses of what is appropriate motherhood can be found – for example, the child-rearing literature, where (often male) experts identify what 'good mothering' is – women are not passive in the process of becoming mothers. Rather, they negotiate what it means for them to engage in motherhood and construct their own identities as mothers that not only takes account of the 'intense mothering' recommended by the experts, but also incorporates their own experiences and pressures to perform in non-family areas of social life – such as work (see McMahon, 1995). However, this does involve mothers in wider social debates about the 'proper' role of mothers in the upbringing of children (see the position of New Right sociologists in Chapter 4). This incorporates contradictory forces in which motherhood is either idealized as a nurturing essentialist attribute for the 'good society', or mothers are 'demonized' if they fail, or see themselves as failing, to measure up to the idealized version of what motherhood is (Glenn 1994). The key element in this contradiction is the increasing likelihood that mothers, even of small children, are engaged in paid employment outside the home. The tension between home and paid work is often presented as a dichotomy in which women either choose between motherhood and contributing to the family income. Garey (1999) argued that this was a false dichotomy and, instead, women 'interweaved' work and mothering commitments into packages of activities that best suited their circumstances and their longer-term ambitions for both family life and outside work. This was not a new phenomenon, as women had continually managed home commitments and survival activity throughout history – what is new is the social insistence on the separation of motherhood from wider social formations like work (Hrdy 2009).

In the sociological consideration of motherhood, the children themselves are often taken as given and ignored as active agents in the construction of what it is to be a mother. Cultural anthropologists have identified a large number of variations in the patterns and processes of mothering along lines of culture, ethnicity, class and so on (see Barlow and Chapin 2010). Part of this variation emerges from the interactions between mother and child in which they try out their own strategies with each other, rather than the children having 'mothering' thrust upon them. Mothering practices are therefore not simply some sort of template that the mother applies to the children; they are intersubjective practices, in which both children and the mother explore the meanings associated with the actions in which they mutually engage (LeVine 2007).

Teenage parents

Becoming a parent as a teenager has almost exclusively been seen as negative and a 'problem' in society. It is typically portrayed as a catastrophe for the individual concerned, their family and society at large. Those who become very young parents are often seen to have pathological problems. Politicians and the media have been the most vocal critics of early parenthood. They have pointed to a decline in moral standards, a breakdown in family life, a burden on the welfare state, poor prospects for such parents in gaining employment, and the poverty and cultural deprivation for the child as consequences of such behaviour. In the 1990s, Conservative politicians, in particular, argued that young women who had few prospects in life were deliberately having children as a means to gain council housing as a priority group. Although this idea was widely debated, especially within the media, there has been little research evidence to substantiate the claims. The commonly held view that the numbers of teenage parents is increasing is also not substantiated by the figures. Research by the London School of Economics and Political Sciences (2010) found that there had been a fall in teenage pregnancies since the 1960s. According to Duncan (2006), in 2004 only 12 per cent of conceptions were to women under the age of 20, and even smaller numbers to women aged under 16. Indeed, sociologists have argued that there has been a moral panic around the threat posed by teenage parents to the 'traditional' family. There are a number of areas that must concern us as sociologists about these public debates. First, was there ever a 'golden' age of the family? How can we compare figures with the past when the 'shame' of teenage single parenthood would have meant cases were undetected and hidden from view? How far are the media responsible for citing unrepresentative cases and thereby fuelling the moral panic?

According to research by Alexander *et al.* (2010) there is little, if any, evidence to support the 'ignorance–calamity–social problem' picture of teenage pregnancy and the social policies – such as the setting up of the Teenage Pregnancy Unit to halve the numbers of the under-18 conception rate by 2010 – which have arisen related to it. The media are responsible for presenting a stereotypical image of young mothers as 'dysfunctional'. Mollborn and Lovegrove (2011) argued that this image was, in part, responsible for the very limited research that has been carried out on teenage fathers, partly because they are less likely to be co-resident with the mother of their child, but also because of popular perceptions of teenage pregnancy being a problem about teenage motherhood. They found surprisingly few differences between the attitudes of teenage fathers to their responsibilities, compared with adult fathers, despite the lower incidence of co-residence. According to Bell (2004) and Duncan (2006), teenage parenting might, for some, be more of an opportunity than a catastrophe. First, when poor outcomes for mother and child are predicted, there has been no consideration of the variations experienced by different groups, young mothers are compared to *all* mothers and there has been no control for differences in class and ethnicity. Second, becoming a young mother may not *cause* poor outcomes such as poor education, income and employment prospects. Rather, young motherhood and poor outcomes maybe caused by *social disadvantage* prior to pregnancy (Duncan 2006). So, becoming a teenage parent may be part of a wider constellation of social disadvantage that existed before the pregnancy and continues after. Small-scale qualitative research has also found that many young mothers have positive attitudes towards parenthood, making them feel responsible, mature and able to cope with their new role. Other research (Phoenix 1991) found that early motherhood was a turning point in life, with women returning to education or employment and becoming determined to be independent and provide support for their child(ren). As a consequence, self-esteem, security and stability improved in their lives. Alexander *et al.* (2010) also point out that teenage pregnancy is not necessarily a result of ignorance concerning contraception or low expectations, according to their research.

Other factors to consider are class and ethnicity. The public views expressed about teenage parenthood may be more closely associated with the middle class. For working-class women, becoming a mother at an early age may be quite compatible with expectations in community and family networks. The support from family and friends may also be available in such communities. Furthermore, the educational and employment phenomenon. Similarly, grandchildren will increasingly have their grandparents alive and taking an active role in their childhood, and sometimes into their adult life. This has repercussions for intergenerational family relationships and has been an under-explored area of sociology. However, the subject has been part of some research conducted by Clarke *et al.* between 1999 and 2002 to explore the role of grandparent in families (ESRC 2003).

Structured interviews were used with a small sample of grandparents, which also allowed respondents to give open-ended answers to the majority of the questions. This was followed up with secondary analysis of the interviews, exploring themes that arose about the experience of grandparenting and ideas about how grandparenting should or should not be carried out. Mason and Burke (2010) report that new norms regarding the role of grandparents are being developed and negotiated. The first of these is 'not interfering'. This seems to mean that grandparents want to present a united front along with the parents of their grandchildren, so that children received consistent and clear messages about how they should behave and the rules by which they are expected to live. Second, good grandparenting was about 'being there', giving unconditional support on a range of issues to help with the care of grandchildren. These issues could be about everyday life, or being 'on call' to help out in emergencies. On the other hand, grandparents also felt the need to have their own time and time off from family duties to explore their hobbies and interests. But they also wanted a balance of intergenerational family relationships to complement this independence.

Conjugal roles: a postmodern evaluation

The ideas of Parsons, and Young and Willmott, while presenting a different image of family life and roles, can be seen as modernist, in that they are based on the idea that there is a 'normal', 'natural' or 'best' form of the family and the relationships and roles within it. This modernist image is associated with the idea in sociology that absolute truth exists and can be revealed by sociological inquiry. Therefore, a 'best form' and a 'most common form' of the family exists – and this is how it should be!

Postmodernists take issue with the idea of absolute truth in society. They argue that all knowledge is relative and that all claims to truth are as valid as each other. According to this view, since family forms and family relationships are varied, there is no such thing as a 'common family', or even a 'best family'. Anything goes! In the postmodern era, it is individuals who make sense of their familial and post-familial relationships, and use a variety of relationships beyond the realm of the family to help construct their own sense of identity in society. Some postmodern thinkers see this fragmentation and dismantling of the nuclear family as a force of liberation, whereas others see it as a source of chaos. These views will be discussed in more depth later in this chapter.

Decision-making in the family

For Stephen Edgell (1980), the idea that roles and relationships in the home are becoming increasingly more democratic and symmetrical is not supported by contemporary sociological evidence. Edgell suggests that the family is still essentially patriarchal in nature – even middle-class families, which are often seen as the seed-sowers of domestic equality.

Item A

Money, marriage and ideology: holding the purse strings?

According to evidence from America there has been a fundamental change in the old marriage bargain of men being the breadwinners and women being the housewives, mothers and home makers. The Pew Research Centre in Washington DC has shown that the proportion of American wives earning more than their husbands has risen five-fold since 1970. The majority of these wives are also as well or better educated than their husbands. One of the authors of the report describes this as a 'portrait of gender reversal in marriage' (D'Vera Cohn 2010). In 1970 only 4% of wives earned more than their husbands but by 2007 this figure had increased to 22%. Although in one in four marriages men are still the bigger earners. American sociologist Andrew Cherlin says the findings indicate a fundamental shift in marriage over recent decades – to a dual-earner family pooling resources and creating better off families. The shift is underlined by the fact that unmarried men, who once had the benefit of not having a family, have now fallen behind. The report also points to the women's growing financial status having an impact upon power realities in the family especially in relation to major purchases and household finances. High earning women seem also to be more likely to make most decisions about household finances and expenditure.

The Pew study is based on US census statistics for married couples aged between 30 and 44 and charts the reversal in patterns of education within marriage. The evidence points to the link between the changing financial situation and rising levels of education among women. The 1970s were an era of increasing educational benefit for women and this is reflected in their financial prowess and clout.

Cherlin adds that in the past men were uncomfortable and insecure about wives who earned more and indeed fifty years ago would have been ashamed if their wives worked, Now 'they are pleased and less pressured than a generation ago' about these changes.

Source: *The Guardian* (2010).

Exercise 7.7

Read Item A, and answer the following questions:

1. Explain in your own words why women's earning potential is increasing.
2. Find out if women are earning an equivalent amount to men in the UK.
3. Do you think more equality in financial matters in the households leads to equality in other areas? If so, why?
4. Why is there a link between education and women's earnings?
5. Do you think women generally have higher aspirations than in the past? Compare the current generation with the previous one.

social actors for the 'family ideal' of the private, warm and secure nuclear family, under postmodernity this ideal is exposed as ideology. The ideal of the nuclear family has come crashing down around us, and all that there is left to do is to construct an individual identity, to develop individual lifestyles. As family life has changed – increased cohabitation, later marriage and childbearing, more people remaining single, divorced and re-partnering – would it be appropriate to say friends are the new family? With the increased emphasis on choice and individualization, perhaps families now play a less important role in providing care and emotional support for members. Certainly, it is true to say that there is considerable diversity in our experiences in families. According to Allan (2008), gay and lesbian networks are 'families of choice', whereby the family is less about blood ties and kinship and more about long-term commitment. In trying to understand how lesbian mothers and gay fathers redefine their family practices, in his research in Norway, Folgerø (2008) found that couples simultaneously reproduced heteronormative assumptions about fatherhood, motherhood, family and kinship, but also transgress these assumptions in the way they conduct their lives.

Is there postmodern choice?

For Jon Bernardes (1997), an author influenced by some postmodern ideas, the transition from modernity to postmodernity has led to familiar liberation. He argues that the contemporary postmodern family relationship is characterized by choice, freedom, diversity, ambivalence and fluidity.

This mirrors the ideas of Cheal (1991), who suggests that the postmodern era is based on chaos and pluralism – the fragmentation of previously taken-for-granted forms of family life in favour of more individualistic responses to lifestyle construction. A similar image of the postmodern family is provided by Stacey (1990), who considers that contemporary family relationships are 'undecided'.

As with the claims made by interpretive sociologists – with whom we opened this chapter – from a postmodern perspective, Bernardes (1997) suggests that family lives are a product of lived reality. They are not fixed or static – we cannot think about 'the family' as a thing, as a structure. Instead, we should talk of 'family practices', since the only real thing about the family is that it involves individuals engaged in action. This postmodern preoccupation with the diversity of social forms and lifestyles will be explored further in Chapter 8.

According to Bernardes, we 'make' or 'construct' families through the following actions:

- the sharing of mealtimes
- keeping a sense of history through photographs and albums and so on
- by playing games as children and with children as adults ourselves
- negotiations about TV viewing and home computing
- decision-making and negotiations about bedtimes
- power relationships based on the form of talk and discourse known as 'nagging'.

ⒾⒶ

Exercise 7.9

This exercise extends the idea of negotiation in relationships. In Exercise 7.2, we saw how a couple may negotiate the details of their marriage relationship. Here, we shall apply this notion to the relationship between parents and growing children.

As you grew up, the relationship between yourself and your parent(s), or those in a position of parental responsibility, gradually changed over the years. In most cases, this will have meant that you gradually gained more rights and power over your own actions as the older person(s) relinquished this power. However, we are sure you will agree that this process often involved some 'battles' between all those concerned.

As a group, discuss how this actually happened in your case, and compare your experiences. You might, for example, compare what you were each allowed to do at the age of six with what was allowed at the age of 16. You should find differences not only between these two ages, but also between individual experiences at each age. Some of the areas of negotiation you might discuss are bedtimes, TV viewing, domestic chores, clothes, going out, tidiness and so on.

What are 'family practices'?

To return to the work of David Morgan (1996), a fuller explanation of the concept 'family practices' is needed in order to explain the nature of relationships within families in what Morgan sees as the postmodern age. Morgan, who has been influenced by the French sociologist Pierre Bourdieu (1990), suggests that families are 'practices' because:

- they are created by individuals 'doing' interaction – therefore, by looking at what people actually do in families, we can get closer to the viewpoint of those engaged in creating families
- they are highly active, not fixed
- they involve a sense of the everyday nature of ordinary, common-sense life
- although they are active and dynamic, they are nonetheless a regular feature of life, even in the postmodern age, but in different, increasingly more fragmented forms than under modernity
- they are active and regulated, but they are also fluid; they are open-ended
- they can be located in both the history of the entire social system, and in the personal and unique individual biographies of those involved.

Morgan's concern with structure and action are mirrored in Giddens' idea of structurational sociology.

Strengths and weaknesses of postmodernism

Strengths

- postmodern ideas allow sociology to explore the individual meanings that social life has for those involved (much like interpretive sociology). rather than making massive generalizations and sexual partnership offer today – divorce, HIV/AIDS and so on. Equally, however, the family might provide a safe haven from these risks.

ⒾⒶ

Exercise 7.10

We can also analyze marriage and sexual partnership in terms of the 'risks' described by Ulrich Beck (1992). The decision to marry or form a long-term partnership involves considerations of freedom, personal choice and power. Draw up an extended version of the table below and fill in the boxes with your own list of the risks that might be involved in such a decision, together with a list of the ways in which family life might provide protection for the individual. We have provided some examples to start you off.

Risks as part of family life

Risks that may be faced in marriage/long-term relationships	Protection provided by marriage/family life
The stress of possible divorce	A safe haven from outside stress

ⒾⒶ
(An)Ⓔ

Exercise 7.11

Beck and Beck-Gernsheim (1995) suggest that the decline of the traditional family has left a vacuum of chaos in family relationships. In the absence of other yardsticks with which to measure relationships, more pressure is likely to be put on the quest for romantic love and marital/family relationships based on this.

You can investigate this concern by carrying out a content analysis of a number of problem pages. An explanation of how to carry out such an analysis was provided in Exercise 7.5. Problem pages can be found in a wide range of magazines, tabloids and even quality newspapers (although perhaps not always in the same form).

- What evidence can you find to illustrate the lack of clear norms and 'yardsticks' in the measurement of the quality of relationships?
- What sort of worries do people express?
- Do they seem to be trying to measure themselves against some sort of imaginary standard or ideal?
- Are there examples of other readers writing in with their own experiences and advice?

Exam focus

How can the postmodernist perspective be used to undermine traditional sociological approaches and theories of the family?

Key areas/questions to address in planning an answer are:

- The notion that all knowledge is relative and that there are no certainties and absolute truths in the world are central tenets of the postmodernist view – how does this relate to the family?
- For postmodernists, the conception of a dominant or 'ideal' form of family would be questioned, as the postmodern world enables choice, individualism and diversity.
- How far does the evidence of family change and diversity support the postmodernist argument?
- Does the conception of the family as fragmented and individualized fit with the statistical evidence or your experience of patterns of household living?
- How would feminists and Marxists reply to the postmodernist? Is there a place in our theorizing about the nature of the family for sociological theories such as these?
- Has the nature of power in the family really changed? What evidence can you provide that men are still the dominant force in family life?

Important concepts

Individualization • Heteronormativity • Gay and lesbian households • Structuration • Conjugal roles • 'Display' • Cultures of intimacy • Co-parenting

Critical thinking

1. Does the evidence suggest that the demise in traditional family values has been exaggerated (see Scott 2006)?
2. Discuss the ways in which friends are taking over some of the more intimate and personal roles previously carried out within the confines of family relationships.
3. Has the 'pick-'n'-mix' family arrived? Do we make choices about how we form our family relationships depending upon our needs at any one time? Would your own experience support this argument?

more choices, flexibility and a whole range of options for family living. In order to make sense of the wide variety of family forms, they argue that sociologists need to look at five types of diversity:

- *Organizational diversity*. Different family types have different structures or ways of organizing the household. In some families, only the husband goes out to work; in others, the wife is the sole wage earner; and others are dual-worker families where both partners earn a wage. These organizational differences can have massive implications for the day-to-day life of the family in question and, in particular, how roles are performed and by whom (see Chapter 7).
- *Cultural diversity*. The nature of family life can vary considerably between different ethnic and cultural groups.
- *Class/economic diversity*. Class can contribute to family diversity. For example, Young and Willmott (1975) believe that middle-class families are more likely to share domestic roles and be 'symmetrical' than working-class families (see Chapters 6 and 7).
- *Life-course diversity*. The nature of the family can change over the life-course of the individuals. For example, we can expect family life for a newly-wed couple in their early twenties to be different from that of a couple in their late sixties whose children have left home and now have families of their own.
- *Cohort diversity*. Individuals born in the same year ('cohorts') may have similar experiences of family life due to their common experience of wider social and historical events.

ⒾⒶ

Exercise 8.2

Having read about the types of family diversity outlined by the Rapoports, copy and complete the table below, and think of several examples for each category of diversity. We have provided some examples to start you off.

Type of diversity	Examples
Organizational	(a) 'Reconstituted' families may have a range of different relationships
Cultural	(a) Cypriot families often live in extended family groups
Class/economic	(a) Upper-class families are more likely to have help with child care from a nanny
Life-course	(a) A couple who are in their fifties are likely to live alone as their children have left home
Cohort	(a) Children born in the 1970s and 1980s are likely to stay at home longer than those born in the 1950s, partly because of the lack of jobs and the end of university grants

Now write a paragraph outlining the nature of the family and family relationships today. Use some of the statistics you have found and conclude by evaluating the Rapoports' work on family types. What are the differences between family organization and arrangements since 1982?

It is worth noting, however, that some commentators stress the overwhelming similarity and popularity of a specific family form over time. It has been suggested that there is a '*neoconventional family*' (Chester 1985). This means that – despite moral panics about family decline, break-up and crisis – most individuals find a partner, marry and have children, and most of those who divorce seek to remarry. Scanzoni (2004) argued that, in the United States, there are still numerous social signals that the 'standard family' is superior to other family forms, which are lower down a 'pecking order' of acceptability.

Equally, it must be remembered that, even if household formations vary in size and structure, kinship patterns may still flourish outside non-traditional household arrangements. For example, Peter Willmott (1986, 1988) argued that three main types of kinship pattern could be identified in Britain:

- *Local extended family*: two or three nuclear families, who live in separate households but see each other often and live in close proximity to each other.
- *Dispersed extended family*: nuclear families, who see each other relatively frequently, but not as regularly as the local extended family. They live much further apart. This could apply to many ethnic communities who maintain international connections with their kin.
- *Attenuated extended family*: similar to the dispersed extended family, but the contact between members is even less frequent.

Research in Swansea by Charles *et al.* (2008), which aimed to update earlier research by Rosser and Harris in the 1960s, has found that the three-generation extended family living under one roof had declined from 1 in 5 families in 1960 to 1 in 200 in 2003. The only section of the population where the three-generational family remains is the Bangladeshi community, which is the largest ethnic group in Swansea.

It is worth noting here that arguments about family diversity may simply boil down, in the final analysis, to competing definitions of what we actually mean by 'the family'. As Gittins (1993: 155) states:

> There is no clear, unambiguous definition of what a family is – indeed, it has been argued that the family is little more than an ideology that influences and informs the ways in which people interact and co-reside with one another.

For example, sociologists have used a great range of terms to classify different types of family living. Below are 14 family types, although the list is by no means complete.

- local extended family
- dispersed extended family
- attenuated extended family
- nuclear family
- neo-conventional family
- reconstituted/blended family (see Chapter 2)
- lone/single-parent family

constructions in advertisements and the architecture of houses. The discourse regarding families is imbued with the notion and ideology of heteronormativity. This makes discussion and debate about variety in family life difficult to divorce from such an emotional agenda. Young single parents are vilified, even though there is some evidence that they cope remarkably well and use the birth of a child to stimulate their education and career path to best support their children. Gay and lesbian parents are seen as 'unnatural', despite their maturity in ensuring their children develop well educationally and as emotionally stable adults.

Childless by choice

While there is a growing number of couples in Western societies who follow their life course without ever having any children, the situation of childlessness is sociologically complex. The decision not to have children might be temporary, or a 'permanent of the moment', or permanent. That is, at any moment in time, a couple may put off having children with the intention of having a family later in their life course, or have decided not to have children but retain the option of reproduction by keeping their fertility potential, or have committed to childlessness through medical procedures. There are many sociological explanations of the choice to remain child-free, ranging from cost-benefit analysis – where there is a rational calculation of the cost (both economically and emotionally) to a couple of having children, to life course explanations – which focus on the life experiences of individuals (such as experiencing parental marriage breakdown at an early age) as indicators of later decisions to remain child-free. There are also factors such as ethnicity and religious beliefs which, in the United States, have been shown to have an effect on the probability of voluntary childlessness (see Bulcroft and Teachman 2004). In the United States, the proportion of African-American women who are childless has grown, although it is difficult to determine whether this is a choice, or as a result of other factors (see Tucker, 2000). In the United Kingdom, Gillespie (2001) argued that there were 'active' and 'passive' deciders amongst women who chose childlessness. The former were more likely to be responding to negative experiences earlier in their lives, whilst the latter were not attracted to the image of motherhood in a strong way. However, the strong ideological push of 'pronatalism' that is present in Western societies tends to frame these decisions in some sort of deviant enclave, with an assumption that those who chose childlessness will somehow come to regret this in later life (Morell, 1994). However, a study of childless couples in the Netherlands found that the lack of a support network in later life was not detrimental to the couple, as there were financial resources available to provide substitutes (Dystrka and Wagner 2007).

Stepfamilies

With the increases in divorce, cohabitation and remarriage, there is a consequent increase in the incidence of stepfamilies, or re-constituted families. Sociological interest in such family formations has increased as the proportion of stepfamilies in the population has become larger. Initially, research into stepfamilies deployed a deficit model, in that the benchmark for 'success' in such marriages was the idealized nuclear family of a life-long relationship. Analysis of stepfamilies therefore took place in comparison to the nuclear family, the results of which tended to find that stepfamilies had higher levels of tension and were not as good at solving problems (Bray, 1988). However, sociologists were also at pains to establish that there were different forms of stepfamilies and they could not all be treated as an undifferentiated mass. Burgoyne and Clark (1984) identified different types of stepfamilies, distinguished by their perceptions of their own circumstances. These ranged from those who did not perceive themselves as a stepfamily at all; through those who celebrated their differences from 'normal' families; to those who wanted to be as like a normal family as possible, but for whom the tensions and conflicts within their situation made this difficult.

More recent research focused on the dynamics within stepfamilies and used more qualitative techniques to explore the negotiations that went on amongst reconstituted families. Amongst many, a key finding was that women had more say in financial decision-making in their second families than they had in their first (Burgoyne and Morrison 1997). Research by Hetherington (see, for example, Hetherington and Kelly 2002) into the relationships between stepchildren and their step-parents revealed some interesting sociological processes going on, some of which seem common-sensical and others more surprising. For example, it was found that a step-parent was expected to take fewer responsibilities for the stepchildren than if he or she had been the biological parent, but that step-parenting girls was more difficult than step-parenting boys, regardless of the gender of the step-parent. Step-parenting teenagers was also more fraught than with younger children. One of the key elements in generating animosity from stepchildren towards a step-parent is the perception by the stepchild that they are being treated unfairly compared with the biological offspring of the step-parent. This also illustrates an important aspect of stepfamilies, which is that they are not of all one type. Stepfamilies in which there are the biological offspring of both remarried parents experience more complex inter-relationships than those where only one of the step-parents has children brought into the marriage. The existence of an involved biological non-resident parent also complicates the situation of the reconstituted family.

Feminist views on family diversity

Barrett and McIntosh (1991) argued that the existence of family diversity stands as a direct criticism of the reality of the ideology of the family. They suggested that, since there is no common form, how can we say which family type is 'best'? The ideology of the family suggests that not only is the traditional nuclear family the best way to live our lives, it is also the most common. In fact, these two factors – frequency and suitability – are often confused. The ideology tells us that the nuclear family is the most frequent because it is the one that is best-suited to our needs. However, as evidence on the great diversity of family forms indicates, there is no single common form – and therefore, argue Barrett and McIntosh, no means by which we can judge one form to be better than another.

Some feminists value family diversity as a liberating force for women in society. The existence of widespread diversity means that women might be able to choose which type of family to have, and therefore determine their own lifestyle options. This view is held by the feminist thinker Gittins (1993) and, in some respects, it is similar to the postmodern

- traditional nuclear family
- juvenile delinquency
- responsible for its own members
- single-parent families
- control and discipline
- cheap local authority housing

TYPES OF DIVERSITY

Diversity and location

Eversley and Bonnerjea (1982) identify six different areas in Britain, each of which offers a different type of family organization, thus contributing to family diversity:

- *the affluent south of England* – mobile, two-parent families where the children move out at an early age
- *coastal areas of England and Wales* – elderly and retired couples who may be living apart from other relatives
- *industrial areas* – traditional working-class families with a strong sense of both community and family in old, declining industrial areas based on traditional industries such as coal mining
- *families coping with life in recently declining industrial areas* – which are rapidly and recently experiencing unemployment in areas such as the Midlands
- *rural areas* – families who work in agriculture and related areas of the economy, and tend to be of the extended family type
- *inner cities* – a large turnover of mobile families plus single person households, multi-adult households and lone parents.

Eversley and Bonnerjea suggest that different life experiences, shaped by different geographical locations, lead to very different experiences of family life, and therefore great diversity.

Exercise 8.6

- How could you bring Eversley and Bonnerjea's types of family organization linked to geographical area up-to-date?
- What has changed since the early 1980s?
- How might the economic climate in the 2000s differ and thereby affect family diversity?
- What about the ethnic and cultural differences that exist in these geographical locations?

Culture and diversity in the UK

Early research into family diversity in Britain included descriptions of different cultures and ethnicities, and the variations in family patterns. Examples are usually, but not exclusively, drawn from white British researchers. Ballard (1982) was interested in the differences within South Asian families, and between these and white British families, and noted that many families of South Asian origin have a strong sense of family and community due to the experience of migrating to Britain. Whereas many first-generation family members are highly conservative, protecting their traditional culture in the face of the host Western culture, British-born generations may challenge some aspects of their traditional culture.

The influence of ethnicity and culture upon the family might lead to a diversity of family types within the same ethnicity. For example, some British-born Asian couples have rejected the traditional patriarchal family structures, whilst others are based on very separate roles and an extended family model, perhaps further divided into smaller supporting groups. As Ballard notes, British-born South Asians have experience of two very different cultures: the traditional culture within the family home, and the wider culture experienced outside the home – for example, at school. Research for the Joseph Rowntree Foundation by Salway and Chowbray (2009) and Hauari and Hollingworth (2009) suggests that men in a number of different minority ethnic communities (Pakistani, black Caribbean, black African, and Asians from a variety of ethnic and religious backgrounds) are adopting close and loving relationships with their children, and see their role as fathers very differently from previous generations. They are now multi-dimensional roles that take on the emotional and care-giving aspects of parenting previously seen as the domain of mothers.

Oakley (1982) studied Cypriot families living Britain and found that such families often perform an economic function (see Chapter 2), with the different generations working together and offering support in the face of 'society outside'. This supports Ballard's claim that migrant families, in order to cope with the experience of settling into a new culture, often re-enforce their traditional ideas and values and, in so doing, offer a safe haven from an often hostile and sometimes racist wider society. Many black feminists – such as Amos and Parmar (1984) (see also Chapter 4) – suggest that, for some black women, the family offers much more comfort and support than it does for white women, since black women need a place of refuge away from racist society.

Jocelyn Barrow (1982) suggests that although West Indian families in Britain might appear nuclear in structure, if we look at the actual power relations and life experiences within the home itself they are, in fact, very different from the traditional notion of the nuclear family. Barrow notes the existence of 'mother households' amongst some West Indian families, where the wife is the breadwinner and neighbours – who may or may not be part of a wider kinship network – help out with communal childcare and other community projects, such as preschool groups.

These studies tended to make comparisons with the traditional versions of families that existed in the migrants' country of origin, or with family organization of the 'host' culture. Few viewed the family from the perspective of the migrant or ethnic group, which may well have given a different account of family life. Furthermore, the accounts given of these families were very much 'looking from the outside in', and did not try to understand or explain the family life of the members and wider kin who remained in the country of origin.

Research in the 1990s has been of a more qualitative nature, using in-depth interviews, case studies and an ethnographic perspective to gain insight into the family life of those involved. For example, Bhatti (1999) carried out research with Asian families from different religious traditions using in-depth interviews with 50 families and found the existence of strong loyalty to family ties, family honour and emphasis placed on trying to maintain

3. What effect has the rise in divorces had?
4. How does support from the state make lone parenthood more possible today?
5. Why do motherless families make up only a small proportion of total lone-parent families?
6. Why do some women today choose to have a child/children but choose not to marry?
7. Why are some women today more able to make this choice?

TOWARDS A 'NEW ACTION THEORY' OF FAMILY DIVERSITY?

For some sociologists, family diversity allows sociology to investigate the amount of freedom and free will that social actors may or may not have in society. For example, for postmodernists, diversity is liberating, as it offers choice to the individual. On the other hand, for those on the New Right, the family is often seen as a structural constraint on individuals, rather than a product of their own action. For example, it might be tempting to see single-parent mothers as the victims of absent fathers. We must realize, however, that all family alternatives, including lone parenthood, can involve deliberate lifestyle choices and are not just something 'done to' the individuals involved 'from above'. Single parents, for example, may actively choose this lifestyle due to their financial situation. They have their own money and, therefore, independence from the other parent. They are able to make their own decisions without having to rely on the other parent. This realization that actors (in families, as elsewhere) have 'agency' – or free will – in making choices in their lives, leads us to consider the issue of diversity in interesting sociological directions using new theoretical tools. For some thinkers, the answer to studying family diversity and free will within the family is to use structurational sociology – or, as some commentators have called it, the 'new action sociology'.

Structurational sociology (see Chapter 7), as developed by Anthony Giddens, is concerned with unifying (drawing together) both ideas of social structure and human action. Two statements made by Giddens when outlining his theory of structurational sociology are important for our purposes here:

> social practices, biting into space and time, are considered to be at the root of the constitution of both subject and social object. (Giddens 1984: xxii)

> Human agents or actors – I use these terms interchangeably – have, as an inherent aspect of what they do, the capacity to understand what they do while they do it. The reflexive capacities of the human actor are characteristically involved in a continuous manner with the flow of day-to-day conduct in the contexts of social activity. (Giddens 1984: xxii–xxiii)

What Giddens means is that humans create society through their actions with each other in society and then pass this reality down the succeeding generations as a 'ready-made' reality – or, in other words, as having the appearance of social structure, of a society 'out there'. In acting, we, as the next generation, aware of our actions and motivations whilst performing them, engage with this reality and reform it for ourselves and those who follow us, and so on. Thus, action takes place over both time and space, and action and structure are fundamentally related; one does not exist without the other.

For example, the majority of us are born into families that are ready made – they existed before we were born. At the moment of birth, we have before us a set of kinship relations based on blood ties or step-relationships – or, in some cases, a combination of the two. Whilst growing up, as a member of this ready-made family we contribute to the life of the family. We act and interact with other family members. We follow the family rules at some times, and break them at others. Due to our actions and interactions with other family members, family life changes; it would not be the same if we acted in different ways. Therefore, the family is both a structure that existed before our birth and a product of our own action – we help to shape and mould its precise nature as we act out our lives.

Structures such as the family appear to exist outside our control, and are both enabling and constraining. They limit some possibilities but, in doing so, they open up others. Giddens himself uses the example of sexuality in the contemporary Western world. In a lecture given on 4 December 1995 at the Manchester Free Trade Hall, Giddens argued that the transformations in attitudes towards sexuality that have occurred have liberated individuals from traditional family values, leaving them much freer to explore their sexuality in ways that were previously deemed 'deviant'. Thus, the construction of one's sexual self-identity has become much more a matter of lived choice, as have more general examples of family alternatives and diversity.

Following the ideas of Giddens, Scanzoni (1993) argues that the new action theory can be used to explain other features of family life. He suggests that families are not 'objectively real' – able to be measured 'out there' in society. They are not 'things' that exist around, above and beyond the individuals involved, but are made by them, by their choices, decisions and actions.

Family diversity can be best understood – within this structurational view – as the result of meaningful and creative actions initiated by ordinary people to help them figure out and make sense of the world they live in, their place in this world, their relationships and their own self. We make an active choice in deciding what family form to live in, and in making this choice for ourselves we are also making a choice for our children – the next generation, who, when the time comes, will themselves have to make choices about family life.

Exercise 8.9

The debates on postmodernism described seem quite complicated, but most of the writers are focusing on the same issues – they are just doing so in rather different ways. Below is a list of statements, taken mainly from the latter parts of this chapter. They all fall roughly into one of three categories:

- statements that are modern in approach
- statements that are postmodern in approach
- statements that show the need for a wider view, allowing for some element of each.

Sort the statements into these three categories and then write a summary of the various perspectives used.

2. Your second task is to answer a sample examination question. Read Item A and write an answer to question (a). You might look back to the earlier work on ideology before this part of the exercise, as this element is again very relevant (Chapter 2).

Question

(a) What sociological arguments and evidence can be presented to support the claim that single-parent families 'are not seen as normal or desirable'?

Student answer

What follows is an answer by a student. However, the paragraphs have been jumbled up and your task is to arrange them in logical order.

Paragraph 1
Government policy is a major factor that sociologists point to when looking at the treatment of single-parent families. Much of this policy has been brought in by the New Right. They see the family as the building block of society and see the current 'disintegration' of the family as the result of increased acceptance of other family forms. They see single parenthood as linked to the welfare state – that is, women get pregnant to get a flat. This presents a completely negative view of single-parent families and is totally unsupported by the evidence. John Perry, a housing director, says that in 1993 he could not find a single council that gave precedence to single-parent families. Also, single parents living on benefits tend to have poor living conditions and be in poverty – hardly anything for which to aim. It has also been found that many single parents do not want to be reliant on benefits; they want to work but find it impractical. It has also been found that most single parents do not see their situation as ideal – thus, the parents themselves do not seem to see their situation as normal or desirable.

Paragraph 2
There have also been many theories and concerns about the 'dangers' of single parenthood. In 1993, John Redwood claimed that 'the natural state should be the two-parent family caring for their children'. Murray saw the single-parent family as the cause of the underclass, and many have seen it as causing crime and delinquency amongst the young.

Paragraph 3
Other sociologists have questioned the view that single-parent families are undesirable and a social problem. Some actually see them as an indicator of social progress – that is, showing women's independence. For the main part, however, single-parent families do seem to be seen as not normal or desirable. The name of the charity 'Families need Fathers' says it all.

Paragraph 4
Therefore, most sociological arguments and evidence do support the claim that single-parent families are not seen as normal or desirable.

Paragraph 5
More sociological evidence comes from Johnson, who looks at school hours and holidays, and says that this prevents single parents from working and also two-parent families from both working, thus discouraging anything other than the traditional nuclear family. Marxists would say that the needs of capitalism include the traditional nuclear family, thus supporting the view that they will support it.

Paragraph 6
Much of government policy seems to perpetuate the myth of the wonderful, normal nuclear family. The setting up of the CSA has appeared to encourage fathers to be responsible for their children. However, Abbott and Wallace see this as mainly a finance-saving procedure for the government, as mothers lose benefits if the fathers pay maintenance.

Paragraph 7
There are many sociological arguments and evidence to support the claim that single-parent families are not seen as normal or desirable. Allan says that government policy is based on an implicit ideology of the traditional nuclear family and that this can discourage new forms from developing.

Paragraph 8
However, E.E. Cashmore has questioned the assumption that children need two parents. He says that it may be better for a child to have one caring parent than one caring and one uncaring, especially if there are many arguments. He also says it may appeal to women wanting to escape or avoid the 'dark side' of the family and male dominance. However, he points out that women then become dependent on the state, so he concludes that women do not need a partner so much as a partner's income.

Paragraph 9
More examples of policy are making unemployment benefit unavailable to 16- and 17-year-olds – assuming that the family will take care of them. Care in the Community is another government idea which assumes that the family – and usually the woman – will care for their elderly.

Paragraph 10
Advertising is another source of this, not only in the way it is done, but also what is being advertised. The nuclear family is always shown as being happy and positive – definitely something for which to strive. This is then reinforced by the products: 'family' cars, 'family'-sized packs of food, 'family' holidays, four-chaired dining sets, three-piece suites and so on. The family is always the nuclear, patriarchal one; other forms do not seem to be considered families.

The order in which these paragraphs were originally written was as follows: 7, 1, 6, 9, 2, 8, 3, 10, 5, 4. However, this is not fixed and another order might be appropriate. By the way, this answer would have been awarded full marks.

3. Your final task in this section is to answer the following question:

Assess the contribution made by feminist sociologists to an understanding of the changing structure of the family in modern society.

Divorce is not, however, the only change taking place in contemporary Western family life, and it is perhaps useful to think of divorce as just one of many changes, for example:

- cohabitation – especially in Western Europe – is on the increase, particularly amongst the young
- we have the rise of 're-constituted' or 'blended' families based upon step-relationships
- family members are living longer, which may put increased pressure on relationships and partnerships
- homosexual and lesbian relationships are becoming more open and commonplace, and are given the same civil rights as heterosexual relationships
- family size, in general, is decreasing
- there is an increase in the Western world of single or lone parenthood.
- a decrease in marriage rates in Western Europe and the United States
- households containing non-blood related people – for example, couples with children produced through IVF treatment or adopted
- an increase in 'singleton' households.

Many in the media – especially the New Right – see the rising divorce rate as an indication of a lack of morality in society, and use this as an explanation of juvenile crime.

REASONS FOR DIVORCE

First, we should note that family break-up is not the same as family breakdown. When a family *breaks up*, the members cease to live in the same household – they often go their own separate ways and try (as much as possible) to cut past ties. However, when families *break down*, they stop functioning as a harmonious unit; the relationships within the family – and, in particular, the relationship between the husband and wife – no longer work. Frequently, breakdown eventually leads to break-up. Divorce should not be equated with the quality of marriage or family life either, because the end of a marriage may be more do with the breakdown of a relationship with a partner rather than being a statement about the 'institution' of marriage. Divorce is often the prelude to forming another monogamous relationship and most divorcees go on to re-marry. Hence, there is the increasing use of the term *serial monogamy* to describe our patterns of marriage in the twenty-first century.

Divorce is seen as putting a great strain and pressure on the couple in question, and there is a temptation, in common-sense thought, to see divorce as an indicator of a mistaken, or perhaps even damaging, relationship. Divorce, however, can also be damaging to others involved – in particular, young children. So much so, that we often hear of married couples staying together 'for the sake of the children'. However, research in the United States has found that, in about 40 per cent of divorces where children are involved, they are better off after separation rather than continuing to live in a situation of open and chronic conflict between their parents (Amato 2001). Divorce also severely disadvantages women and children economically (Walzer 2009). The New Right (see Chapter 11) certainly sees divorce as a potential problem for society. Equally, the New Left in the Blair Labour government, elected in the UK in 1997 and the Conservative/Liberal Democrat government's policies from 2010 also placed great value on marriage – as demonstrated in the Green paper of 1998, *Supporting Families* (CSJ 1998, see Chapter 11). The Labour government of the early 2000s introduced the Sure Start scheme, which aimed to provide guidance for parents from pregnancy through to when the child starts primary school. Sure Start Centres exist around the country and bring together child care, early education, and health and family support particularly for those in poor communities and those experiencing fractured families.

Feminists have seen divorce as a way in which women can escape from hostile or patriarchal relationships; a way of regaining control of their lives. Over three quarters of divorces are instigated by women, which proportion suggests their increasing reluctance to remain in an unhappy or unsatisfactory relationship.

General reasons for divorce

- Changes in the law on divorce have made divorce easier to obtain. For example, the Divorce Reform Act 1970 allows divorce on the basis of the 'irretrievable breakdown' of the marriage.
- Divorce has become more socially acceptable.
- Young people who have high expectations of marriage might divorce at a later stage, if these expectations are not met.
- The increased awareness of women's rights might make more women file for divorce as society now expects them to be treated much better by their partners than in the past.
- Longer life expectancy might mean that, as married couples grow older, they grow apart.
- Increased economic pressure (from unemployment and so on) may place an added strain on some married relationships, leading to divorce.
- The 'privatization of the nuclear family' and its geographical separation from extended kin may mean that, when pressure and anxiety hit a marriage, there is less support available and, as a result, married couples are less able to work through their differences.

Ⓚ Ⓤ Ⓐⓝ Ⓔ

Exercise 9.1

A number of factors have been suggested for the increase in divorce in the twentieth century. But exactly why have these factors had this effect? For this exercise, you need to think carefully about how societal changes might have impinged on the individual or couple. Below is a list of factors involved in the rise in the divorce rate. You should think about, or discuss, each of these in turn and write an explanation of the way in which each has affected the divorce rate. Try to put yourself in the place of an individual person or couple – how might this or that factor affect you personally?

- changes in the laws on divorce
- changing position of women in society
- longer life expectancy
- less support from extended kin
- decline in religious authority
- greater social and geographical mobility
- stress on romantic love and sex
- growth in incidence and acceptance of divorce.

- allow for the fact that individuals might interpret their unique realities in different ways – whereas, for some, divorce might be psychologically damaging, for others it might promise future happiness and self-expression
- acknowledge the different ways in which individuals perceive their family lives.

An E

Exercise 9.4

Although divorce is often cited as evidence of the diversity and fragmentation of postmodern life, there are discernible patterns among the factors that seem to be associated with divorce. In each of the cases below, the divorce rate is higher than the national average. See if you can answer the following questions, individually or as a group.

1. Teenage marriages are twice as likely to end in divorce as marriages of those in their twenties. Think of four reasons why this should be so.
2. Those who have already been divorced once, or who have parents who were divorced, are more prone to divorce again. Why should this be? Don't people learn or determine to 'do better'?
3. There are still a significant number of divorces that take place around or after 20 years of marriage. What reasons can you suggest for this? Why bother after all that time?
4. Partners whose status or social backgrounds are different experience higher rates of divorce than average. Why should differences in religion, status, ethnicity or age influence the chances of divorce?
5. Certain occupations have higher divorce rates than others. Those who are away from home a great deal, or are very involved with their work are particularly prone (e.g. prisoners and company directors). Why is this so? Can you suggest some other occupational groups who might be predicted to have high divorce rates? (See if you can find out whether your predictions were correct.) Actors and film stars are famous for their frequent visits to the divorce courts. Can you suggest why they may be more prone to divorce than other occupational groups?

Divorce and reflexivity

Anthony Giddens (1991b) suggests that divorce offers both opportunities and anxieties; it can be liberating – since it allows individuals to chart new directions in their lives, but it can equally be a source of personal disruption, tension and even psychological damage.

Giddens himself cites Wallerstein and Blakeslee (1989), who argue that divorce offers both disturbance and the opportunity to 'grow emotionally'. A key development in the life of divorcees is the process whereby they 'reclaim' and 'rebuild' themselves after the divorce. Hence, through self-reflection, divorce offers the opportunity to think about the nature of relationships, one's own emotional well-being, the nature of contemporary society and the nature of one's own identity. Divorce offers the chance to reconstruct a sense of who we think we are, through an assessment of the risks and uncertainties of contemporary living.

Item A

Cockett and Tripp (1994) claim that family break-up is now a normal feature of family experience. The growth in divorce has certainly had a great impact on family life, and the vast majority of people now know a number of families or couples who have experienced divorce, even if they have not gone through a divorce themselves.

As part of a reflexive process, divorce is seen by others (e.g. Wallerstein 2000) as an opportunity for people to develop their identity and grow emotionally, as well as being a source of great disruption to identity, particularly for children of divorced parents. Indeed, much of the pro-marriage lobby stems from longitudinal research conducted by Wallerstein, a clinical psychologist, which argues that there are negative consequences for children in marital breakdown and divorce.

However, some sociologists argue that, because this change is so sudden and so recent, as a society we have not yet developed clear norms about the type of behaviour that is appropriate. They believe that divorce is not yet fully institutionalized in our cultural structure, and because of traditional attitudes towards and ideology on marriage, many divorcees still feel a significant degree of guilt and failure.

In societies where divorce has traditionally been easy, it may be accepted that a wife and husband will return to their families of origin as a matter of course. This is unlikely to be seen as appropriate in Britain today. So, what is appropriate?

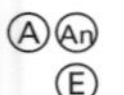

Exercise 9.5

Study Item A and hold a group discussion on, or write an account of the difficulties faced by divorcees – and their friends and relatives – after the divorce has taken place. Are there any 'rules'? If so, what are they? If appropriate, use your personal experiences to explain how you and your family managed divorce. You should consider the following:

- Are extended kin expected to give any help (material or emotional)?
- Where do the two ex-partners now live?
- Unlike the death of a spouse, in the case of divorce others are not sure how to respond – do they offer sympathy or congratulations? (Divorce cards?!)
- Do grandparents have any right to see their grandchildren, who may no longer be living with the grandparents' child?
- What role should a divorcee take up? Can people go back to behaving as they did when they were single? How do they go about finding a new partner?
- How do divorced couples behave towards each other?
- What about arrangements made for children and access to their parents?

Giddens (1991b) has argued that the increase in divorce is part of the general and wider development of a 'reflexive modern' society, rather than a postmodern one. By 'reflexive modernity', Giddens means that we, as individuals in society, come to think in a much

COHABITATION: AN ALTERNATIVE TO MARRIAGE?

Cohabitation refers to couples who form households without going through a legal ceremony of marriage; in many Western societies, including Australia and Canada, the proportion of cohabiting households has been increasing since the middle of the twentieth century. The pattern is common to many Western societies, though it has been longer established in Nordic countries such as Sweden (Andersson 1998). Sociologists have been interested in the meaning of this trend – for example, exploring whether cohabitation is mainly the forerunner of marriage, or whether it constitutes a rejection of the idea of marriage itself (Seltzer 2004). While these alternative explanations of cohabitation have a powerful effect in framing sociological debates about cohabitation, further research revealed that the patterns of cohabitation were more complex than this dichotomous view would suggest (see Manting (1996) for research into Dutch cohabitation patterns). For example, not all cohabiting couples intend to move towards marriage, although many expect to do so (and, in heterosexual couples, women more than men). Cohabiting couples may result from situations where one or both of the couple is still married to someone else and that may or may not lead to remarriage. There are also differences between ethnic groups in the United States, with black women more likely to be cohabiting than white or Hispanic women (Bumpass and Lu 2000).

Another important aspect is that cohabiting couples are more likely either to have children together, or to be bringing up children from previous relationships in a cohabiting union. Indeed, the imminent birth of a child is a spur to cohabitation, as many couples move into together when the woman becomes pregnant (Raley 2000). As a result, increasing numbers of children are being brought up in households where the adults are not married. The effects of this on the children have been the subject of a great deal of sociological research, not all of which comes to consistent findings. Broadly, it would seem that the children of cohabiting couples are hardly disadvantaged at all by their parents' lack of a marriage certificate. However, children brought up in a cohabiting household where one of the adults is not the biological parent are more likely as teenagers to have more behavioural problems (see Manning and Lamb 2002). However, the research also suggests that socio-economic factors and the durability of cohabitation are important factors in children's well-being, with those cohabiting couples with lower incomes and unions of shorter duration producing more teenagers with social problems (Hao and Xie 2002).

THE FAMILY TODAY AND TOMORROW

When studying patterns of illegitimacy, marriage, divorce and remarriage in contemporary social life, we are led – by the very nature of the material – to consider the future of the family itself. As we have already seen, for the New Right the divorce figures represent a crisis for the family: on the other hand, for many of those influenced by a postmodern perspective, divorce, single parenthood and remarriage represent family diversity which, in turn, represents increased choice over one's life – a force of liberation.

The remainder of this chapter will consider the future of the family. We start by noting that the family (however defined) is a constant feature of day-to-day life for many people and, as such, stories of family controversies appear again and again in the media. The family is a source of debate and discussion for politicians, policy makers, lobbyists and religious groups. It is a massive site of socialization, lifestyle choice, identity and consumption. The family is also a frequently explored (and exploited?) topic for moral panics. Given this, family sociology is seen by many as an essential component of sociology courses.

Studying families and households, and trying to understand their contemporary realities and possible future directions, however, presents many problems for sociologists:

- It is a private area of people's lives and therefore not easily accessible for research. Many people in society do not wish sociologists to pry into their very private lives.
- It is held within 'common-sense wisdom' (perhaps through the successes of its own 'familiar ideology') as a natural feature of human societies. It is seen by many as the best way to live.
- The family is considered to be above criticism by many of those with a powerful voice – the media, politicians and religious groups. It is a special part of life.
- The reality of family life is often complicated, there being (as argued in Chapters 8 and 9) a diverse range of family/household types.

Such is the critical nature of sociology that these problems represent a good case for studying the family in the first place. Many discussions on family life are concerned with the future it may take, but this is difficult to assess reliably. Although many sociologists try to adopt a scientific approach towards their studies, following the Weberian argument we could suggest that any attempt to predict the future of human social behaviour is doomed to failure. Humans act and construct reality on the basis of meanings that are open to reinterpretation and redefinition over time (a point reflected in Giddens' work). We also find that marriage is entered into after a period of cohabitation or after children are born, not before. It may also be that the norm of women working is having an effect upon the nature of marriage and divorce. At present, we are still unsure about the precise nature of the family *today*, let alone what the family will look like *tomorrow*!

How can we understand the reality of the changing family?

All we seem to have are a number of ideas, a number of theories – both classical and contemporary – and the observation that there are a great variety and diversity of families and how they operate. These are, though, the essential building blocks of all sociological analysis.

For both the New Right and the New Left, the future of the family is something to be protected and conserved. For postmodernists, the future is seen as characterized by increased diversity, fragmentation and plurality. This is seen by some as providing a successful framework through which to view the future of the family – a future of freedom and choice.

For both the New Right and New Left (but for slightly different reasons), diversity, fragmentation and 'anything goes' is precisely the sort of so-called 'freedom' that leads to increased social problems – crime, disobedience among the young, the spread of sexually transmitted diseases, poverty and the lack of a work ethic. According to this view, the attitude that 'anything goes' is wrong because individuals and families should have some sort of moral responsibility.

The feminist agenda, along with other radical or critical approaches, has provided sociology with an alternative way to view family life: not a life of warmth, security and freedom, but one of oppression and captivity for many women. Freedom and diversity in the future of the family would thus be welcomed by many feminists, but not perhaps in the same way as a 'postmodern freedom'. 'Anything does not go', as patriarchy might continue to exist in a postmodern society where it is impossible to have any truth or morality about life in general, and the family in particular.

The value of such sociological theorizing on the nature of family life is to make unfamiliar that which we often mistakenly take for granted, and to offer fresh ways of thinking about society and our own lives in society. Family sociology stresses a number of factors:

- There exists a powerful ideology of the family in society.
- The family may not be a safe haven for all its members.
- The family is a prime source of ideological socialization.
- There exists a great diversity of family forms as a result of divorce, increased remarriage and cohabitation.
- Marriage, and other forms of family relationship, are ongoing and meaningful constructions that make sense to those who create them.
- There is a great deal of pressure on people in society to accept family life as normal and natural.
- The family is important to life, given the vital functions it is seen to fulfil.
- During the course of the latter half of the twentieth century the nature, size and role played by the family underwent considerable change.
- For many people in society, the 'family ideal' is still an aim or goal in their life.
- The family is an important mechanism for the control of the body and the regulation of sexuality.

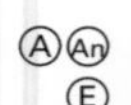

Exercise 9.7

Take each of the bullet points raised in the text and relate each one to the theory or sociologist most likely to make the argument. Explain in your own words the argument they would offer.

The uncertain future of the family

The 'sphere of the intimate' of marriage and the family is a powerful and important aspect of social reality and a mechanism of social control, precisely because it is often central to who we think we are – our self-identity, our own personal 'biography'. However, we also create our identities from interaction with others – such as friends who are outside of family relationships. Ulrich Beck and Elisabeth Beck-Gernsheim (1995, see also Chapter 7) argue that a new *zeitgeist* (spirit of the times) has developed in society. We are living in so-called 'new times' where the reality and future of marriage and the family are up for question. As they comment:

> The nuclear family, built around gender status, is falling apart on the issues of emancipation and equal rights, which no longer conveniently come to a halt outside our private lives . . . If this diagnosis is right, what will take over from the family, that haven of domestic bliss? The family, of course! Only different, more, better: the negotiated family, the alternating family, the multiple family, new arrangements after divorce, remarriage, divorce again, new assortments from your, my, our children, our past and present families. It will be an alliance between individuals as it always has been, and it will be glorified largely because it represents a sort of refuge in the chilly environment of our affluent, impersonal, uncertain society, stripped of its traditions and scarred by all kinds of risk . . .
>
> To put our theme another way, it is no longer possible to pronounce in some binding way what family, marriage, parenthood, sexuality or love mean, what they should or could be; rather, these vary in substance, exceptions, norms and morality from individual to individual and from relationship to relationship. (Beck and Beck-Gernsheim 1995: 2, 5)

For Beck and Beck-Gernsheim, as demonstrated by the quotation, the future of the family as we know it is uncertain. Looking into the future, there are a number of pathways that family life can take. This sense of uncertainty is not just the province of sociological theorizing, however; it is also a fundamental part of the reflexive thinking used by individuals to understand their world – an argument also presented by Giddens. For Beck and Beck-Gernsheim, the future of family and marriage will not involve widespread or total rejection of the family but, rather, a better, more equal, more reflexive type of family.

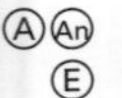

Exercise 9.8

The American sociologist C. Wright Mills has suggested that the value of sociology is its 'sociological imagination': allowing those studying the subject to think in new ways about their society.

Think about all of the ideas, debates, arguments and theories you have studied in this book.

1. Explain which theory you find most convincing concerning the way the family operates in society, and why.
2. Which of the 'uncertain futures' of the family presented in this book do you agree with and why?

Exam focus

Many of you will be required to sit formal examinations during your career as a sociology student. These may be A-level exams or undergraduate exams. The same guidelines apply to these situations, and below is a list of key points to consider when you are preparing for assessment. One or two of the points may seem obvious, but examination markers will attest that they have experience of many candidates who are not successful because they have 'forgotten' a golden rule once under pressure in the examination situation.

1. Read the wording of the question(s) carefully to find out roughly what aspects of the topic are being asked about.
2. De-code the question by underlining useful phrases and command words. Note down the main aspects of the content.
   Take a good five minutes over this – it will help you in the long run. You may be able to spot the parts of the question(s) that will be of most use in your answers and work out how you can use them to best effect.
3. Note down studies and research that are relevant to the question(s).
4. Note how many marks are allocated to the question(s) and gear the length and detail of your answer accordingly. Many students waste time on long answers when very few marks are available, or provide only a paragraph or two when what is required is more like half an essay.
5. Work out which skills are being tested. This will also help you to determine what you must do in your answer. Make sure you know how to display your sociological knowledge, and give examples or elaborate to show your understanding. Most essay-type questions also test skills of interpretation and application, and evaluation, so it is important that you demonstrate these skills rather than providing a list-like, content-based answer. Refer to Chapter 1 for definitions of these words.
6. Note the key command words – describe, identify, explain, discuss, assess, evaluate – of which, in your preparation for assessment, you should know and understand the meaning.
7. Now, at last, you can turn to the questions and write down your answers. It is very difficult not to do this as soon as you open the paper in the examination room – you may feel that you need to write things down straight away before you forget them! However, your initial research and analysis of the question(s) will help you, and your answers will benefit from this more thorough approach.

Have a look at the following exam questions and apply the guidance given to them in points 1–7. You do not need to answer the questions but, rather, assure yourself that you understand the question, de-code it, identify key command words and decide what skills are being indicated.

1. Assess the claim that the increase in the divorce rate after World War II was mainly a result of changes in the law.
2. Discuss the reasons for the increase and decline in the divorce rate in recent years.
3. Outline and evaluate the contribution of feminist perspectives to our understanding of changes in family roles, relationships and divorce.

Important concepts

Reconstituted families • Blended families • Singleton households • Reflexive modernity • Privatization of the family • Empty-shell marriage • Serial monogamy • *Verstehen*

Critical thinking

1. Now that the divorce rate has stabilized or declined, can we argue that the family has also become more stable?
2. 'The more common blended families become, the more likely we are to see our families and family life as fluid and flexible, involving relationships beyond the boundaries of blood kin.' Discuss.
3. Is there such a thing as the 'postmodern family? What would be its distinguishing features?

AGE AS A SOCIAL CREATION

Berger and Luckmann (1967) argued that culture creates for us a great deal of what we take for granted within common-sense thought as 'real' (see Chapter 7). In other words, our norms, values, attitudes and beliefs are a product of the culture that is socialized into us as individuals and which we all share in common. From a phenomenological stance, and working within a micro tradition of sociological inquiry, Berger and Luckmann suggested that the way we live our lives, and the attitudes we have and share with the rest of society (norms and values), are a product of negotiation between individuals. We create, as social actors, the *nomos* (meaningful reality) within which we act and interact.

In the case of age and its related concept of 'generation', we experience, as lay social actors (as 'ordinary people'), stages in our life in relation to what we see as biological givens – changing bodies, hormones, health and so on. Hence, we tend to think of age-groups as 'natural' – babies, children, adults. The result of much historical and sociological inquiry is the notion that, although they do have some basis in human biology, the concepts of age and generation are still social constructions – they are a product of cultural socialization. This point is self-evident in the relatively recent creation of the 'teenager', a notion uncommon before World War II and even more recently the 'tweenie' (young teenager).

The social construction of age and the experiences of different age groups changes over time and across different locations. For example, *adult* understandings of children's lives do not necessarily reflect the lived experience of childhood itself.

Strengths and weakness of the phenomenological approach to age

Strengths

- It concentrates on the role played by meanings and motives – by culture – in the construction of notions of age
- Their ideas can be used in combination with cross-cultural and historical materials to provide evidence that notions of time and age are culturally created.

Weakness

- It over-emphasizes the importance of action and culture while ignoring the role played by structure in the creation of age – for example, economic factors involved in health care may contribute to increased mortality rates, and thus help to create what we mean by age.

ⒾⒶ

Exercise 10.2

Before reading about age as a social construction, you should spend some time thinking about our expectations regarding age and how it affects our perception of people's behaviour. Working in a small group, each group should divide a large sheet of paper into four. As a heading for each quarter, insert the ages 2, 15, 40 and 75. In each of these sections, write down a list of the characteristics you would expect of people of that age – you know nothing more about them, only their ages. Some of the things you might consider are their behaviour, attitudes, dress, hair, interests, status, treatment, rights, activities, leisure pursuits and so on. What things would be true of one age, but not true of another?

When you have completed this activity, compare your results with each other. Did you write similar things?

Now discuss the following questions:

1. Are these characteristics typical of this age group because the others are unable to do these things?
2. Switch around the ages on your sheet. How silly do the characteristics look when applied to a different age group? What would happen if a person behaved in the manner expected of someone of a very different age?
3. What common stereotypes emerge within the groups – e.g. old age?

By now you will have begun to acquire some idea of the social construction of age.

Calendar age and time

In Western culture, when we talk about the age of an individual we mean the chronological time (in years) that has passed since she or he was born. However, it is important to note that in non-Western cultures age is sometimes measured by the passing of events, rather than the more abstract concept of time. For example, age may be measured in relation to the spread of a great disease, a flood or some other natural occurrence.

Calendar time is intimately bound up with the onset of Western scientific rationality and, ultimately, the development of the capitalist economic system. Time, in the Western sense, argues Norbert Elias (1992), is a source of both social order and social control – it is the cement that binds society together:

Calendar time illustrates in a simple way how the individual is embedded in a world in which there are many other people, a social world, and many other natural processes, a natural universe. By means of a calendar, one can determine with great exactitude the point at which one entered the flow of social and natural processes (Elias, 1992: 28).

Age gives the individual their sense of identity in society. In the West, we tend to think of wisdom coming with the progress of age, and the young are seen as inexperienced and relatively low in status. In other societies, and in the past, the young were powerful and revered.

Age, then, is a social construction – as are notions of time. So great and powerful are these two controlling and regulating mechanisms in the Western world, however, that they occupy a very special place in common-sense thought. They are accepted without reflection.

> In the more developed societies it seems almost self-evident, for example, that a person knows how old he [sic] is. Members of such societies react with amazement, or perhaps head-shaking incomprehension, when they learn that in other societies there are people who are unable to give any definite answer when asked their age... [in the

in more recent times by the New Right, particularly in respect of their attack on lone mothers, who in their view are unable to exercise correct discipline over their children (see Chapter 11).

The anthropologist Matthew Speier (1976) offers an alternative to the traditional sociological account of the socialization of children in the family. He suggests that children are all too often treated in the sociological literature and wider society as blank sheets of paper – creatures that are in need of socialization from adults in order to make them fully functioning members of their culture. According to this view, we too often ignore the highly creative world views of children – the worlds of play, imagination and games, through which they attempt to make sense of the world being presented to them by powerful adults.

Speier notes that traditional sociological ideas about the family led socialization of children to operate within what he calls 'five main ideological conventions':

- children are 'adults in the making'
- children are 'made into' adults by adults themselves
- children's development into adulthood is progressive and is about learning how to be 'competent' in the world
- unsuccessful socialization results in the child growing up to be a 'deviant'
- children are seen as defective in their social participation, since they have not yet learnt, by virtue of their being children, how to behave in the adult world.

For Speier, this means that sociological discussions on the role of children in the family are clouded by the very same ideological and common-sense theories used by society's adults in the family home. He suggests that we – as sociologists – should examine this ideology of childhood socialization, rather than just taking it for granted. Perspectives on childhood are beginning to emerge that question the power relationship between adults and children. Why do we assume the adult is guiding or socializing the child? If we look at the behaviour from a different angle, we could say that adults control children and use their powerful position to define childhood. The popular TV programme *Supernanny* is an example of these two perspectives on childhood. It could be viewed as an 'expert' helping parents get unruly children under control and behaving in a socially accepted manner through the use of sensible rules and sanctions. However, it could also be viewed as adults having the ultimate controlling power over the behaviour of children and using forceful means to get them to comply with adults rules of what is acceptable childish behaviour.

Exercise 10.4

Speier argues that thinking of children as blank sheets of paper, to be written on by adults through socialization, is a very limited view. Children have their own world, which they construct partly through play, and are not passive but are creative in making sense of the world. Use Ridge's ideas about children as active social agents to provide further critical examples.

Look again at the 'five main ideological conventions' described by Speier and for each one provide:

1. an example of some aspect of childhood that illustrates that particular convention
2. a contrasting example of some aspect of childhood that illustrates the idea that children have their own views, have conflicts with adults and create/negotiate their own world.

THE SOCIAL CONSTRUCTION OF CHILDHOOD

The term 'social construction' refers to the ways by which we, as a society, give meaning to something – in this case 'childhood'. We assume childhood is a natural state of being but, in fact, we can show that, sociologically, children's experiences are far from common even in a single society and vary enormously globally. Although (as with old age) our common-sense notions of childhood portray this stage of life as regulated by calendar time and biology, we should not see it as a universal or biological given. It is a product of human culture. Consider, 'childhood' implies dependency upon others, not just physically and emotionally, but also economically and legally. However, there are many examples of 'children' who in other parts of the world are acting as adults – caring for their siblings, earning money, looking after sick adults, maintaining a home, working, fighting in wars. In the UK, according to the 2001 Census, there were an estimated 175,000 young carers who were responsible for looking after their disabled, sick or infirm parents, and running a household whilst also going to school. Thus, our notions and perceptions of childhood are at odds with the real experiences of many children, Not only are these massive social constructions, they also change over time and space. For example, at 16, 18 and 21 transitions are made from childhood to adulthood, as set down in law. There are restrictions on the age at which you can work, get married, have sexual relationships and so on. Thus, although our childhood is seen as a biological entity, and a matter for our private family lives, it is in fact regulated by the very public face of the law.

Common-sense notions of childhood are based on notions of 'separateness'; we define what children are like by what they are not – they are not adults and they are separate from the adult world, yet they will join the adult world at a later stage in the life course.

This 'ideology of childhood' views children as different from adults. They need to be cared for, protected and helped, and taught how to be an adult – the assumption being that without the correct training, children will somehow grow up 'wrong' or will develop into 'faulty' adults in some way. This is at the heart of the functionalist emphasis on the importance to the child of family socialization, as reflected in the work of Parsons.

It is the cultural assumptions our society makes about the nature of children's bodies that leads us to treat them as separate from the adult – as vulnerable and in need of care, and dependent upon the wider adult world. Since children's bodies are seen as immature and undeveloped, it is necessary for society to place them under massive surveillance and digital media – children are becoming increasingly exposed to images and messages that were seen by adults only.

According to Postman, whereas the medium of printing created what we understand today as 'childhood', digital media are in danger of ending it. With the arrival of mass printing, and especially with the onset of the capitalist economy, it became vital for individuals to learn how to read and write. Whereas once this was just the privilege of the upper and middle classes (often with the help of private tutors in the family home), it now became necessary for the whole population living and working under capitalism. Schools and schooling were therefore created and, in doing so, 'childhood' was invented – representing the process in which one waits to become an adult and learns to become an adult. However, with the widespread influence of television, and more recently digital media, the boundaries between childhood and adult experiences have become blurred. For example, in today's world children watch TV news and witness sights previously thought of as adult-only experiences; they regularly see images of death, war, violence, disaster, famine and so on. Equally, children are now exposed to media images of sex, violence and drug-taking. The 'sexualization' of women and children – particularly in popular culture and the music industry – has had a marked effect upon young girls in their perceptions of themselves and the increasingly 'adult' fashions available to that age-group. In 2010, there was a minor moral panic about the sale of padded bikini tops on sale for seven-year-olds. Primark withdrew this item from their shops after pressure from child protection consultants (*The Independent* 2010). The coalition government of Conservatives and Liberal Democrats has explicitly targeted limiting the 'commercialization and sexualization' of children in their policy pledges on the family in 2010.

Children in the home: the rise of child-centredness

Brigitte Berger and Peter Berger (1983) argued that the origin of the traditional nuclear family lies in the development of the middle classes in nineteenth-century Europe. A key feature of this sort of family structure was the way in which children were treated. It was 'child-centred' because the decrease in infant mortality meant that children became an ever-present feature of the household. They were seen as in need of protection, care, emotional comfort, religious and moral upbringing, and discipline.

Since that time, children have become a prime focus of the family and family life. The 'bourgeois family' has become a private realm of life, away from the public world of the economy and the state, and the focus of this private life is the welfare of children.

Ⓚ Ⓤ Ⓘ Ⓐ

Exercise 10.8

Put together an account of child-centredness in modern society. Make a list of all the ways in which we exhibit our child-centredness, showing the great amount of time, money and effort we put into 'doing our best' for our children and protecting them.

It is also a feature of modern parenthood that we seek advice on child care from 'experts' on matters of health, socialization and child psychology.

1. How do we protect children from the 'nasty' bits of life? What sorts of things are hidden from them?
2. What kinds of 'expert' do we consult to help us to care well (and 'correctly') for our children? (Think about books, magazines, clinics and so on.)
3. How do we cater for children in special ways? You might consider, for example, clothes, toys, food, holidays and so on. You may find that the list is very long!
4. What sorts of 'big business' are involved in catering for children?

The rise of child-centredness could stand as evidence of what Norbert Elias (1978, 1982) called the 'civilizing process'. The ideas inherent in the process do, after all, seek to control children whilst protecting them. And it is certainly true that life for the majority of children in contemporary Britain is a great deal easier than it was for children born to our Victorian ancestors. Elias argues that the history of Western society and culture can be charted as a history of the increased development of this civilizing process. He explains social change as moving along on a path of progression towards the 'civilizing' of all practices in social life – leisure practices, warfare, emotions and personal relationships, to name but a few. To become 'civilized' means the rationalization, monitoring and protection of individuals in society by means of cultural practices designed to regulate and restrain. For example, the concept of table manners – a product of the 'bourgeois family', as described by Berger and Berger (1983) – was developed to regulate and 'refine' human social relations at meal times.

Exercise 10.9

Ulrich Beck (1992) suggests that society puts great pressure on couples to have children, that 'somehow the life of the parent is incomplete without the child'.

Put together an account of the ways in which:

1. couples are put under pressure to have a child
2. couples will go to great lengths to have a child
3. couples will fight hard to hold on to a child.

It could be argued that increased child-centredness serves many of the child's needs but, on the other hand, it can cause problems for the parents. For example, the birth of a child could be seen as a barrier to the individualization process in society, as many parents experience pressure to 'go without' for 'the good of the child'.

Ulrich Beck (1992) described the hold that children can have over adult family members as a 'dictatorship of neediness'. In many societies, so much pressure is put on couples to have children and make the family 'complete' that childbirth is a forced aspect of family life. Beck describes modern children as 'overloved' and a 'final alternative to loneliness'. Indeed, such is the pressure to have children in a relationship, Beck notes, that they sometimes end up as objects fought over in the divorce courts; somehow, the life of the parent is incomplete without the child.

supermarket selling children's clothes and toys to find out the ways in which boys and girls are differently treated.

James *et al.* (1998), in *Theorising Childhood*, suggest four approaches to understanding the nature of childhood that have implications for sociological analysis:

- Childhood is socially constructed – not fixed or true, but different in different cultures. What is viewed as 'normal' is different across the world and in different historical periods.
- Childhood can be viewed ethnographically by trying to understand the language and lives of children from their perspective.
- Children can be viewed as a minority group, relatively powerless and excluded from the adult world.
- Childhood can be viewed as one stage in the life-course along with other stages in the structure of age stratification. There are common features of age categories, similar age friendship groups, tastes, dress, economic status and so on.

YOUTH CULTURE, CONSUMPTION AND THE MEDIA

As well as childhood being seen as a cultural product – a social construction, many also see contemporary notions of the teenage years as a social construction. Consider for a moment the way in which we think about teenagers in common-sense thought, as frequently expressed through the media. Teenagers are seen both as children in adult bodies and as young adults with the emotional dependency of children. Due to biological (hormonal) factors, our society tells us that the teenage years – and the onset of adolescence – are characterized by a number of changes representing a new stage in the life course: spots, tension, anxiety, 'puppy fat' and awakening sexuality. These factors are seen as biological not social, since they have some sort of physiological reality – we can 'see' adolescence taking place and, as adolescents, we can often feel it.

However, for many sociologists, what we regard today as the essential characteristics of a teenager are a historical product created after World War II, with the rise of affluence and the establishment of a popular music industry looking for new consumers for its products. The marketing industry, to some extent, is responsible for identifying teenagers as a distinct group with its own culture, tastes and style. The recent addition of 'tweenies' – young teenagers – to the teenage group is another example of a socially-created age group.

In the postwar years, the period between childhood and adulthood became acknowledged as distinct. Youth became seen as a period of transition recognized as an important stage of development in social roles, responsibilities and expectations. Ariès (1973) argues that adolescence is actually a social invention – previously there had been no transitional stage. Children moved straight into the adult world – in medieval times, at a very young age. There are a number of arguments about why this came about. The period of education was extended because of the need for prolonged training, so that dependency for some became longer. On the other hand, the postwar young workers had greater earning power than the same age group of previous generations and were therefore more affluent. The mass media, fashion and music industries identified a 'new' market in the teenager and contributed to the development of a 'style' associated with that group of young people. Hence, the emergence of a youth culture with its own norms, value and attitudes distinct from the older generation. The Teddy Boys of the 1950s and their successors through the decades have been studied by sociologists as a youth subcultures with their own rituals, lifestyles and symbols. They were perhaps subversive, in that they challenged the codes of behaviour, hairstyles and dress associated with the older generation, and attempted to mark out their own territory as a group. Once again, much of the research about teenagers tended to ignore females, ethnic minorities and the middle class, focusing on white, working-class males. The sociological research was itself somewhat stimulated by white, male, middle-class researchers from the universities of the 1950s and 1960s, who saw their counterparts – working-class, white/black males – as exotic, different and a world apart from their conventional experiences. Hence, there is an inherent bias and cultural 'reading' of these groups from their perspective.

The role of children as consumers in capitalism

As Robert Bocock (1993) noted, in order for Western capitalism to continue, there has to be an ever-increasing consumption of the goods it provides. In order for this consumption to continue, children have to learn to consume, as it is not a natural or biological condition to want or desire the goods offered by the capitalist economy. The family home is often seen as the site where capitalist consumption is learnt – often through socialization by the mass media.

Humans are viewed as symbolic creatures – we manipulate signs as a way of communicating with others, often through the use of language. Given this symbolic basis of human action, for some commentators consumption, too, is a process of manipulating signs. We define who we are by what we buy. If this is the case, we could see early childhood consumption in the capitalist economy as a process of socialization into society itself.

Postmodernists see the consumption of signs as part of the process in which individuals create for themselves a postmodern social identity. Our image of who we are – our 'self' – is constructed through the goods we buy, the signs we consume. A prime site for such consumption is the family home, especially because children demand a great number of goods and products they see in the media, especially at Christmas. Children and teenagers are particular targets for developing consumption patterns that mark them out as different from adults in relation to clothing, music tastes, leisure pursuits, food and so on.

According to Marxists, consumption under capitalism serves only the interests of those who benefit from the way in which the economy is structured: the ruling capitalist class. Childhood consumption has little to do with self-identity and more to do with the manipulation of false needs and desires by capitalism, in order to keep the economy moving. In this view, children are a handy 'market opportunity' – they are easily manipulated purchasers, through their parents. For example, a brief glance at a Saturday morning children's TV slot on a commercial station will indicate the extent of the products provided by the capitalist economy for children and teenagers to consume.

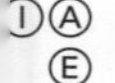

Exercise 10.10

We have looked at a number of different perspectives on the role of consumption and its relationship to age. Postmodernists see the consumption of signs as a part of the creation of self-identity. Marxists see consumption by the family as serving only the interests of the ruling class, as families are manipulated into wanting more and more goods.

Write an account of how postmodernists and Marxists would each see the role of consumption – first, for children; and then for tweenies or teenagers. You will need to answer the following questions:

1. How does the consumption of goods produced by capitalism help the child to form his or her identity?
2. How does the consumption of goods produced by capitalism help the 'teenager' to form his or her identity?
3. How can the consumption of goods by children (or their families on their behalf) be seen as a 'manipulation of wants' and a 'market opportunity' for capitalism?
4. How can the consumption of goods by teenagers be seen as a 'manipulation of wants' and a 'market opportunity' for capitalism?

THE DARK SIDE OF THE FAMILY FOR CHILDREN

Using a more feminist (see Chapter 4) or radical psychiatric (see Chapter 5) approach, we could attack the claim that the family offers some sort of safe haven for all children. This idea is included in the work of Michel Foucault, who suggests that the family is a massive site of social control of children; limiting their development and shaping and moulding them, rather than providing emotional security and love.

Understanding child abuse

In recent years, we have come to realize that child abuse is much more prevalent than we once thought (or wished to think). Or, perhaps, child abuse has always been present but expertly hidden from public view, or ignored by groupings of people with an interest in keeping it out of sight. A notable example emerged in 2010, when the Catholic Church was found to have covered up child abuse carried about by priests over many years. The Pope himself was implicated in the conspiracy of silence over a long period of time surrounding the abuse of children that took place in children's homes and schools in Ireland.

Also, there have been several high-profile cases of child murder that have brought about changes in social policy as a result. The death of Victoria Climbié in 2000 at the hands of her great-aunt brought about the introduction of 'Every Child Matters', a policy that attempted to bring together all professionals who work with children – teachers, police, social workers, health workers, doctors and so on – to ensure that any concerns about the treatment of a child would be identified and could then be dealt with. Unfortunately, in 2007 the death of baby Peter Connolly, aged 17 months, was not prevented, despite the involvement of doctors and social workers in the case on many occasions. His death led to the removal of the head of social services in Haringay, which Ofsted described as 'target driven', and the reorganization of social work departments. However, despite these changes, in 2010 Khyra Ishaq died of starvation at the hands of her mentally ill mother and her boyfriend.

Safeguarding children is now a priority in schools. Teachers and other school staff are trained to deal with children who may disclose ill treatment, neglect or abuse against them. Ofsted inspect the safeguarding procedures in place in schools, and social services departments try to ensure that effective measure are in place to protect children.

However, we must note that, for the majority of children, the home does offer protection and comfort, and that the abuse of children is not a new phenomenon but one that stretches way back into the past. This observation is not meant to be sensationalist; neither does it mean that abuse is acceptable. Clearly it is not, yet it is vital to note that the reality of child abuse must be understood, if we – as a society – are to do something about it.

During the 2000s, we witnessed numerous moral panics about child abuse – moral panics that resulted in children being taken away from their parents and, in some cases, away from children's homes. For a while, the media presented us with images of a society recoiling in horror at the unthinkable – that the abuse of children was widespread and was commonplace. These media images were accompanied by stories of paedophilia and child pornography, especially on the rapidly expanding (but misunderstood) internet. Cyber abuse of children is now widely recognized – whereby adults 'groom' children by tricking them into thinking they are the same age, gender, have the same interests and so on, and then persuade the child to meet them in person. Several high-profile cases revealed the nature of this crime and the fact that networks of paedophiles operate exclusively through the use of the internet to gain access to vulnerable children and teenagers for the purposes of sexual abuse. Little Teds Day Nursery was at the centre of an horrific child abuse case in 2009, when it emerged that a trio of child abusers who had only met on Facebook were involved in recording the abuse of children on their mobile phones. Vanessa George, a nursery nurse, and Angela Allen, who was herself 'groomed' by a male paedophile (Colin Blanchard), took pictures of herself abusing children and posted them on the internet. This was a particularly high-profile example of the nature of this crime.

Measuring the extent and nature of child abuse is by its nature very difficult, because it is hidden from public view and, therefore, an extremely difficult area to investigate.

Steve Taylor (1992) noted that for many the increased number of child abuse cases – as with other crime statistics – represents an increase in reporting, rather than an increase in frequency. However, this tells us nothing about the nature of the abuse. For example, some forms of physical abuse are much more likely to be spotted by outside agencies – teachers, social workers, medical workers, the police – than sexual abuse. Equally, many children may not understand that they have been abused, or, if they do, they may be afraid to speak out about it.

As Taylor indicates, there is some evidence to suggest that some families are more likely to be investigated as potential 'abusers': these families include the working classes and those who have regular contact with the welfare services.

Child abuse also involves a degree of morality (of saying that something is wrong or bad), and this is a cultural construction. Our society has decided – as reflected in the law – what counts as abuse and what does not. Children have been abused throughout history – why then have we taken up the issue today? This is a profitable question for sociological analysis, as it can tell us much about the values of the society we live in, and how such values change over time. It is also a vital question to ask if we are to control abuse; we have to know exactly what it is and why it happens before we can legislate correctly against it.

Item A

Measuring child abuse

Reported cases provide a readily available source of data on child abuse which has been professionally identified. It allows for cases to be followed up and trends to be systematically monitored. However, critics claim that reported cases understate the true incidence of the problem, as many cases of abuse may not be reported or recorded. For example, a child may not recognise what is happening as abuse, or may tell but not be believed, or evidence may be successfully concealed from the investigating authorities.

There is some evidence to suggest that reported cases may provide samples which are systematically biased and, therefore, of little value for projecting guidelines about child abuse in general. First, some forms of abuse involving physical injury or neglect are much more likely to arouse suspicion than sexual or emotional abuse (Finkelhor and Hotaling 1984). Second, families that have relatively regular contact with welfare services or the police are more likely to be 'labelled' as abusers, particularly if their personal characteristics and social circumstances correspond to those on the officials' 'check-lists' (Taylor, 1988). Suspicions that data from reported cases may be seriously deficient, both in numbers and quality, have led researchers to other methods of trying to establish the scope of the problem.

Survey and interview data

Most of those who feel reported cases underestimate the true incidence of child abuse have used 'victim surveys'. Samples of adults are contacted and interviewed, or asked to complete a written survey, the aim of which is to find out how many experienced abuse in their own childhood. In looking at the results of this method, it is important to bear in mind that victim surveys only attempt to 'measure' prevalence; that is, the proportion of adults who claim to have been abused at some time. Obviously, prevalence studies, covering a person's entire childhood, will tend to produce higher percentage figures than studies of incidence, which only attempt to 'measure' rates of child abuse in a given year. This is one of the reasons – we shall see others later – why it is so difficult, and often unwise, to compare the figures of prevalence surveys with reported cases of incidence.

How are we to account for these wide variations? In an analysis of 12 of the major American studies of prevalence of sexual abuse, Peters *et al.* (1986) suggested that the major reason was the different *definitions* of abuse used by different researchers. Whilst some defined sexual abuse in a relatively narrow way, others used a much wider definition including, for example, indecent exposure, sexual propositions and seeing pornography. While these much wider definitions have the advantage of providing data on a greater range of experiences, there is the danger that they may produce findings which are over-generalised. For example, in the definitions used by some studies, the subject who had been 'flashed at' once on her way home from school, the subject who had seen pornography and the subject who had been repeatedly raped by someone charged with her care and protection would all be classified under the same category and included in the same percentage figure. Some researchers have attempted to refine the original definition by distinguishing, for example, between contact and non-contact abuse, but, even then, a term such as 'contact abuse' can cover a wide range of different experiences.

Peters *et al.* found, as might well be imagined, that studies employing a wide definition of abuse tended to produce higher rates. They also suggested that the way in which the data were collected – the methodology – influenced the findings. For example, random rather than selected samples, interviews rather than self-administered questionnaires, tended to produce higher rates of prevalence. On the assumption that concealment of sexual abuse is the major problem, Peters *et al.* advocated that in future researchers should try to use random samples and interviews, as these methods seemed to 'draw out' higher rates. Finally, because prevalence studies are necessarily retrospective, there are problems arising from respondents' willingness and ability to recall things that happened long ago. Response rates tend to be relatively low and we simply do not know whether those who respond provide a numerically high, low or random sample of victims.

It may seem unnecessary to ask what child abuse is. It seems painfully obvious. Child abuse is behaviour such as beating, neglecting and sexually exploiting children. However, no behaviour is *necessarily* child abuse. Children have been beaten, neglected and sexually exploited in the past without people even feeling it was wrong, let alone that it was abuse. For something to be 'seen' as an act of child abuse there must also be a moral reaction from society, that is, the act must go beyond the limits of what is considered acceptable conduct towards a child. These standards change over time and vary between cultures and subcultures. Child abuse is, thus, a product of social definition, because its meaning arises from the value structure of a social group and from the ways these values are interpreted in given situations. From this point of view, the positivist notion of 'true rates' of child abuse which exist independently of varying human definitions of the problem and are waiting to be uncovered by the correct research techniques is an absurdity. It is only because human societies have certain ideas about conduct towards children that they are able to identify some acts as 'child abuse'. In essence, researchers are no different. It is only through their conceptual ideas about child abuse that they can study it. The concepts structure the data. Thus, the statistics of incidence and prevalence are products of the *theoretical* categories in terms of which they are collected. What is being allegedly 'measured' in these studies is a *concept* of child abuse.

Source: Taylor (1992).

Exercise 10.11

Read Item A and answer the following questions.

1. Why are reported cases of child abuse likely to 'understate' the problem?
2. Why might 'victim studies' be a more valid measure?
3. Explain what Taylor means by the difference in rates produced by prevalence studies and incidence studies.

Exercise 10.13

Study Item B and answer the following questions.

1. What proportion of the population was under the age of 16 in 2008?
2. What was the total proportion of the population aged 65 and over in 2008?
3. What is expected to happen to the proportion of those (a) under 16 and (b) over 65 after the year 2008?
4. Explain the different proportions of women and men in the 65+1 age groups.
5. Which age group is predicted to increase most after the year 2008?
6. What evidence is there Figure 10.1 to support the idea that the elderly are becoming a 'burden' on society?
7. What form might the major costs of this 'burden' take?

Exercise 10.14

In rural societies things did not change very much from one generation to another and a person who had reached old age was revered for his or her advice and wisdom.

Retirement, loss of status, cheap tickets and ridicule... all of these show that the elderly do not signify much today.

1. The two statements above reflect very different attitudes. Write an explanation of what each statement means and why the elderly have lost status in modern society.
2. A growing proportion of the elderly is seen as isolated or lonely. Of those aged 60 and over, more than 30 per cent of women and 15 per cent of men live alone. Write an explanation of the reasons for this isolation. (Hint: you could consider the importance of life expectancy, family change, retirement and welfare.)
3. What is meant by 'ageism'? Why is it seen as an ideology?
4. Discuss whether an Age Discrimination Act would be useful. Make a list of advantages and disadvantages.

Old age and marriage

One of the effects of increases in longevity is that many married couples are living together for longer periods of time, and this poses a series of challenges to their relationships. For example, they may need to think about retirement as a joint endeavour, as it may be the first time that they are both in the home together at the same time for significant periods (see Alford-Cooper (1998) for an account of long-lived marriages on American couples). Patterns of working and non-working between husband and wife also seem to affect their responses to dual retirement (Cooney and Dunne 2004). The adjustment to dual retirement works in similar ways for gay couples as it does for heterosexual ones, with the difference that emotional and social support are more likely to come from 'families of choice' amongst gay and lesbian partners rather than children (Cohler and Galatzer-Levy

2000). The state of health of respective partners is important in influencing the level of satisfaction in the marriage that retired partners report (Yorgason *et al.* 2009).

However, longevity also increases the potential of individuals to experience divorce or bereavement. Hatch (2000) argued that the responses of men and women to marital disruption differ according to gender. For women, the loss of a spouse is more likely to create financial uncertainty, whilst for men, losing a wife leads to emotional or social instability. Glaser *et al.* (2008) argued that, as marital disruption through divorce becomes commonplace, then the potential of divorce to undermine intergenerational support to one or other of the aging divorcees is decreased. Differential responses to bereavement by gender may also be explained by the tendency for men to die earlier than women, with the result that there are more widows in the population than widowers. This means that it is often easier for widows to socially integrate into their peer group than for widowers, with the result that greater proportions of widowers report states of depression than do widows (Lee *et al.* 1998). Bereaved individuals may look to remarriage as a lifestyle choice in their old age, as the elderly look for companionate relationships more than younger individuals may do.

Increasing life expectancy, and the rise in divorce and the formation of stepfamilies, also complicates the structure and relationships of multigenerational families (as well as increasing the span of the generations). In terms of relationships between the generations, there have been two main approaches to this complexity. The first draws upon the concept of 'intergenerational solidarity' – that is, that the main feature of relations is that of support and cross-generational assistance. This can operate in both directions – for example, with elderly parents providing financial assistance to younger members, and younger members providing care to the frail elderly (Bengston *et al.* 2002) The second approach uses the idea of 'intergenerational ambivalence' to signal that relationships between the generations can be characterized by both support and conflict, with warm and hostile feelings often being held by family members simultaneously (Connidis and McMullin 2002). Much of the ambivalence centres around differences concerning the degree of independence exercised by younger generations, the degree of dependence that the elderly impose and the role reversal that results from the ageing process. For example, daughters tend to perceive the support they give to their mothers as more intensive than the mothers themselves believe they receive from their daughters (Lin 2008).

Old age in capitalism

According to Chris Phillipson (1982), living in a capitalist society creates particular problems for the elderly – and, in particular, for working-class elderly people. Since capitalism is based on people who are useful to the continuation of the capitalist economy – useful for their labour power – the elderly find themselves in a particularly problematic situation. They are ex-workers, once useful to capitalism but now a drain on its resources through welfare provision.

Looking at successive New Right (see Chapter 11) policies on care during the 1980s, the policies of community care and 'rolling back the state' would certainly serve as confirmation of the claims made by Phillipson, if they were interpreted from a Marxist perspective. The state does not wish to spend vast sums on people who cannot contribute economically

Sörensen 2006). Older women are also likely to be poorer because they will have smaller pensions because of breaks in the working lives to have their children, or having paid the married women's national insurance contributions which only entitle them to a smaller state pension. In Japan, where, despite a fall in the number of elderly who live in the same household as their children, the proportion of the old who express a wish to be cared for by a spouse rather than younger generations has increased, it is still mainly the female elder who takes on this prime responsibility, rather than an elderly male (Naito and Gielen 2005).

Ⓘ Ⓐ Ⓐⓝ Ⓔ

Exercise 10.16

What new insights would feminist sociologists bring to the sociology of the elderly? Think about the gender differences that exist in the experience of old age. Put together an account of the ways in which women experience old age differently from men.

You should include a consideration of the differences in the meaning and impact of retirement for each gender, financial considerations, the role of carer, living alone, health matters and so on.

To what extent have the views considered so far in this chapter been focused on male experience rather than female?

The visibility and invisibility of death in the family

Anthony Giddens (1986) showed that demographic changes (changes in population make-up) in the Western world have had a major influence on family structure and the day-to-day experience of family life for those involved. In particular, the attitude towards death has changed in recent years.

As Giddens notes, the death of a family member was a frequent feature in the life of the pre-industrial or pre-modern family. Death was not confined to those at the end of the life course – that great leveller, epidemic disease, was rife and was not constrained by age. Today, however, death in the family is something we tend to associate with the elderly. Death has become a more or less 'invisible' feature of family life. This raises problems for social actors, as it makes death, as a reality of the life course, harder to come to terms with. Norbert Elias, in his book *The Loneliness of the Dying*, agrees that death and dying have become hidden away from the family. Never before have people died as noiselessly and hygienically as today in these societies, and never in social conditions fostering solitude (Elias 1985: 85).

According to Phillipe Ariès (1981), the rise of the individualism associated with Western industrialization and the rise of capitalism has made the certainty of death more of a problem. For the members of a tightly-bonded family group in the pre-modern age, the potential crisis the death of a family member was likely to cause was submerged by the power of the group. Howeverm we now have the 'privatization of death', where the death of a family member has been taken away from the family and put into the hands of 'death specialists' – under the control of medical power regulated by the state.

Drawing on the ideas of Anthony Giddens and Norbert Elias, Chris Shilling (1993) argues that death in contemporary life represents a major problem for individual self-identity. He suggests that when death was a visible feature of life – in the pre-modern era – it was seen as less of a 'threat' to the security of the individual than it is today. Now, because it is 'invisible', it is viewed as a great uncertainty – something we are unable to come to terms with. The problems of death for the individual sense of security and certainty about life in the contemporary age is a theme explored by Giddens (Beck *et al.* 1994), who suggests that late modernity is a 'post-traditional social order'. It has done away with all the ideas we traditionally took for granted about life, and has left us trying to find new answers to explain the nature of life – and the nature of death.

According to Giddens, in order to solve these fundamental questions about life and death, about the nature of what it is to be human and exist as a human, we create lifestyles around which we can establish our own sense of self-identity. Thus, our 'self' – who we think we are – is largely under our own control: a product of self-definition.

Shilling (1993: 182), taking the ideas of Giddens further, sees contemporary life as 'riding a juggernaut which is out of control'. In contemporary life, we are becoming acutely aware of our own 'unfinishedness', yet the certainty of death – this invisible but ever-present feature of family and individual life – threatens the 'business as usual' of day-to-day life. It calls into question all that we know, and think we know, about life, the family, relationships, the life course and our own sense of who we are.

The elderly in postmodern times

The ideas of postmodernity mean that sociology should reconsider the role that age plays in social life. These postmodern ideas – which are treated critically by Featherstone and Hepworth (1991) – call into question the process that we have called the life course, and suggest that the boundaries between ages and the roles specific to age groups and generations have become increasingly blurred. The main events, which were previously associated with each distinct stage in life, have begun to merge into one another – that is, they have become 'de-differentiated' as age-specific experience declines. A good example of this the numbers of older people who are active, fit and healthy, and are able to go on holiday, take part in many leisure pursuits (some associated with the young, such as running marathons), and family-related activities. In effect, there has been a three-stage shift in the role played by age in the social construction of our reality:

- *Premodern society.* As indicated by the work of Ariès (1973, 1981) and Elias (1978, 1982, 1985), before industrialization and the creation of a capitalist society based largely on the 'privatization of the personal and emotional' and the rise of individualism, people's age was not as important as family status in determining the roles they played and the amount of power they had.
- *Modern society.* With the rise of modernity there was a rise in the importance of chronological age as a factor in role allocation.
- *Postmodern society.* In this view, sociological concerns with the life course are essentially modernist and, as such, are outdated. In this post-modern age, chronological age has become increasingly less important as a factor in the creation of self-identity.

Theorists of the movement towards a postmodern society point to an emerging de-institutionalisation and a de-differentiation of the life course, with less emphasis than

Chapter 11

Families, Politics and Social Policy

By the end of this chapter you should:

- have examined the relationships between the family and social policy
- understand the similarities and differences between the New Right and the New Left
- have explored the views of the New Right and the New Left on the role, importance and future of family life
- have examined the relationship between family policy and welfare policy
- have explored political and sociological debates on the role of single-parent families in society
- have evaluated current family policies from critical sociological perspectives – such as feminism and Marxism

WHAT IS SOCIAL POLICY?

The term 'social' refers to anything connected with or to do with society; the term 'policy' refers to actions taken by a government. Sociologists have long been interested in the role of social policy and the consequences of policy decisions on the society in which we live. The study of the nature of social policy and the family is instructive in showing us the underlying ideology, values, beliefs and views behind the actions of government. In the UK, an example of the match between an ideology and policy actions was evident in the early years of the Thatcher government, where there was a clear message that the family should look after its members – old and young, healthy and sick. Thatcher famously said 'there is no such thing as society... there are families' (Keay 1987). Her government cut child benefit and welfare spending generally; and introduced 'care in the community', whereby long-stay institutions caring for the mentally ill, the disabled and elderly were closed and replaced by care in the home. These policies assumed an 'ideal' family with a working husband and non-working wife to provide the care (Finch 1989).

The 'family' is often central to political debate in Britain. Political rhetoric – media-friendly 'sound bites' and slogans – holds up the family as a safe haven for individuals in society: a basic building block of any 'civilized' and 'democratic' society. We have often heard politicians talk about the importance of 'family values' or even 'traditional family values'. This was particularly true of the Conservative governments of the 1980s and 1990s, but also the successive Labour governments of Tony Blair and Gordon Brown, which led to some commentators finding the differences in policy on the family difficult to identify. After the UK General Election of 2010, the Coalition government formed by the Conservatives and Liberal Democrats pledged to create a more 'family-friendly' society and presented policies that would not have been too different under a Labour government.

UNDERSTANDING POLITICAL RESPONSES TO THE FAMILY

The importance of so-called 'traditional family values' is a key feature in other political debates:

- *Crime and disorder*. Importance is given to 'strong family discipline' to control the potentially rebellious young, with particular emphasis on the role of the father as the key disciplinary figure in the home. The family instils in the young 'correct values' for their later adult life.
- *Education*. In the current climate of 'choice', families are seen as needing to take control of their children's education, making choices of schools on the basis of league tables, and to decide on the future of who should maintain school budgets.
- *Health*. Families are seen as both the cause of some ill-health and the best place to care and provide for ailing relatives, especially the elderly and the mentally ill (such care usually being provided by women in the family home).
- '*State overload*'. The blame for this problem, where too many people claim benefits without a genuine desire to seek employment, is put by some on 'problem families' – a term often used as an excuse to attack single-parent families for being 'immoral'.

Exercise 11.1

We have seen how many politicians hold up the family as an ideal and talk about the importance of 'family values'. In particular, in the text the important role of the family is referred to in the context of crime and disorder, education, health and the problems of 'state overload'.

See if you can find examples of the family being referred to in this way in media reports and analyses of political issues – try to find at least one example for each of the four areas of policy mentioned.

Early social policy and the family

In the UK, the postwar Labour government of 1945 had a particular view of the nature of the family and the roles within it. This is difficult to divorce from the postwar ideology

- men and women – according to their biology – should perform clearly defined and separate roles in the home
- without two parents and strong discipline in a family, social order in society will collapse
- all other living arrangements are 'deviant', and therefore inferior and a threat to society.

Item A

Political party manifestos – past and present

1997

Conservatives

The family is the most important institution in our lives. It offers security and stability in a fast-changing world. But the family is undermined if governments take decisions which families ought to take for themselves... Conservatives believe that a healthy society encourages people to accept responsibility for their own lives... we want to help families to help themselves (Conservative Party manifesto: 'You Can Only Be Sure With the Conservatives': 15–17).

Liberal Democrats

Families, in all their forms, are a basic building block of society. But the nature of families is changing. This has brought new stresses which must be addressed. But it has also brought new attitudes, such as the sharing of family responsibilities, which should be encouraged (Liberal Democrat manifesto: 'Make the Difference': 51).

Labour

We will uphold family life as the most secure means of bringing up our children. Families are the core of our society. They should teach right from wrong. They should be the first defence against anti-social behaviour. The breakdown of family life damages the fabric of our society... Yet families in Britain today are under strain as never before (Labour Party manifesto: 'New Labour: Because Britain Deserves Better': 25).

2010

Conservatives

The Government cannot go on ignoring the importance of strong families. They provide the stability, warmth and love which children need to flourish, and the relationships they foster are the bedrock on which society is built. We are determined to give parents more of the help they need and make Britain the most family-friendly country in Europe. A Conservative government will:

- Work to improve Sure Start and increase the services provided in Children's Centres across the country;
- Provide 4,200 extra Sure Start health visitors so parents can get the expert help they need;
- Introduce a new system of flexible parental leave so parents can share maternity leave between them or both take time off simultaneously;
- Extend the right to request flexible working to every parent with a child under the age of eighteen; and ensure that the government leads from the front by extending the right to request flexible working to all those in the public sector, recognising that this may need to be done in stages;

(Conservative Party manifesto: http://www.conservatives.com/Policy/Where_we_stand/Family.aspx).

Labour

- Help for parents to balance work and family life with a 'Father's Month' of flexible paid leave.
- A new Toddler Tax Credit of £4 a week from 2012 to all parents of young children.
- An expansion of free nursery places for two-year-olds and 15 hours a week of flexible, free nursery education for three and four year olds.

(Labour Party manifesto: http://www.labour.org.uk/manifesto).

Liberal Democrats

A fair deal for families of every shape and size

In Britain today, families come in all shapes and sizes. Liberal Democrats believe every family should get the support it needs to thrive, from help with childcare through to better support for carers and elderly parents.

Liberal Democrats will improve life for your family. On top of our tax cuts to put £700 in the pockets of millions of low and middle-income earners, we will allow mums and dads to share parental leave between them so they can arrange family life in the way that suits them best. We will provide better support for children at risk and young adults to help them thrive. We will restore the earnings link for pensions, and offer respite breaks for carers. And we will protect families from unfair bills. (Liberal Democrat manifesto: available at http://issuu.com/libdems/docs/manifesto?mode=embed&layout=http%3A%2F%2Fskin.issuu.com%2Fv%2Flight%2Flayout.xml&showFlipBtn=true&proShowMenu=true&pageNumber=48)

Coalition government – key family policies

The government believes that strong and stable families of all kinds are the bedrock of a strong and stable society. That is why we need to make our society more family friendly and to take action to protect children from excessive commercialisation and sexualisation (The Coalition: Our Programme for Government: 19).

support it. Evidence from both statistical studies of social outcomes for teenage mothers and the more qualitative evidence from young mothers (and some fathers) about their parenting experiences suggests teenage parenting may be more of an opportunity than a catastrophe (Duncan 2006). According to small scale research, young lone parents see it as important to return to education and gain employment in order to support their children. They often express positive attitudes towards parenthood and their growing competence in their new role. So, the idea of the 'social threat' of lone parenthood is to misunderstand the significance of this as an indicator of family breakdown.

Exercise 11.5

Collect media references to recent moral panics. We have given you a range of examples in the text, such as absent fathers, single mothers, state financing of families, child sexual abuse, lack of discipline, gay and lesbian relationships. Try to find examples of as many of these as possible. Try to compare present 'panics' with those of the past.

Kenneth Thompson (1998) suggested that many moral panics about the nature and future of family life, in both the media and political rhetoric, often involve concerns about the risks *to* family life and the risks *of* family life. For Thompson, this 'language of risk' points to two main reasons for the rise of 'family panics' in recent years.

First, the family is one of the few remaining expressions of 'community'. Therefore, if we sense that the family is being eroded by harmful, outside forces, we feel increasingly exposed to the risks of modern living. For example, if we face unemployment, it might be necessary to turn to our close family for support – perhaps not just emotional, but also financial. However, if the family is not able to give such support, this can make a bad situation even worse.

Second, with the weakening of family bonds, we become worried for our young children, who are at risk from a harsh world and, in turn, pose risks to the world through disobedience. Hence, the young are both *at risk* and *are a risk* – to themselves and others. For example, the young are at risk from 'deviant' adults who might wish to abuse them, but equally they are often seen as juvenile 'deviants' themselves and, therefore, a threat to older, law-abiding adults.

Exercise 11.6

Using your collection of media references to 'moral panics', apply the idea of the family 'at risk' to these. Make a list of the moral panics you have investigated and, next to each one, write an explanation of how it could be analyzed in terms of risks. Which ones would you categorize as illustrating the family's exposure to harmful outside forces? Which could you use as examples of the young being at risk and a risk to others? To help you get started we have reproduced below the list of recent moral panics on the family presented earlier in the text.

- concern about 'absent fathers'
- concern about the sexual immorality of single mothers
- the 'drain' on the state finances by families who are not willing to look after themselves through employment
- the sexual abuse of children
- a lack of discipline in the home, leading to the rearing of violent young people
- gay and lesbian relationships, presented as an 'attack' on the 'natural' and 'normal' family

The idea of the family at risk is a central idea in New Right thinking, to which we shall now turn.

THE NEW RIGHT AND 'FAMILY VALUES'

In 1989, Charles Murray was invited to Britain by *The Times* newspaper in order to apply his views to British society, as well as his American homeland. Murray (1990) has extended his condemnation of the 'underclass' by suggesting that this 'lost generation' is populated by single mothers and illegitimate children. Given the lack of a strong father figure in the home, such children – as young adults – are seen by Murray to lack discipline, morality and a work ethic. These values are transmitted within this underclass from one generation to another through the culture of dependency, the cost being picked up by a state that is already in financial crisis.

As noted elsewhere in this book (Chapters 2, 5 and 7), the New Right supports the 'ideology of the family'. They argue that the 'cornflake packet' nuclear family depicted in advertisements is both 'normal' and 'natural' to human social life and, as such, it is the best form of family organization. Any attempts to deviate from this pattern are labeled by New Right thinkers as dangerous, subversive and likely to lead to the collapse of society.

THE NEW RIGHT AND THE FAMILY 1979–1997

The term 'New Right' has been associated in Britain with Conservative Party policies since the 1979 general election – won by Thatcher. In the United States, the term has also been used to describe the policies of the Reagan administration, along with the expression 'Reaganomics'. New Right ideas have been viewed as both reactionary and radical. This is a socio-political perspective that has become incorporated into the repertoire of different sociological theories about the nature of society. More recently, it has been called neo-functionalism. The New Right have sought to protect and conserve what they see as 'traditional family life' and, in so doing, they have made great changes to welfare provision and the economy – most notably through the implementation of 'free market' ideas. In many respects, the New Right are fundamentalists, as they seek a return to the traditional and, in their view, more moral way of life. Part of this was John Major's 'back to basics' campaign in the early 1990s, which referred to a return to 'family values', and beliefs about appropriate behaviour and roles in the family and beyond.

'Ethical socialism': single parenthood

The issue of lone parenthood can be used to analyze further the New Left's ideas on the family. As well as communitarianism, the New Left is influenced by a number of writers who call themselves 'ethical socialists'. This group includes Norman Dennis, and A.H. Halsey. Halsey (1986: 183) comments that:

> there is nothing more important than the policy pursued by the state towards the family ... [mothers] are an essential element of the social division of labour but, unlike nurses, teachers, social workers, and the like, are excluded from the paid occupational division of labour ... The family is our best carrier of the basic education of each new generation of citizens. An enlightened social policy should recognise this and define the experts and specialists, the schools and the child services, as agents for the support, not the replacement, of family upbringing.

Once more, then, we return to the ideological image of the family as 'normal', 'best' and 'essential' for society, and the maintenance of stability in society! Feminists might take issue with this ideological standpoint, since it includes the notion that child care is a job for mothers.

In their book *Families without Fatherhood*, Dennis and Erdos (1992) argue, as do the New Right, that lone parenthood has negative consequences for the overall stability of society – especially if the lone parent in question is the mother. They argue that absent fathers deny children a strong disciplinary figure, which can lead to crime and delinquency in society.

New Labour policies: *Supporting Families*

In November 1998, the Blair government published a green paper on family life entitled *Supporting Families* (CSJ 1998). This was the clearest indication so far of New Labour's position on the role of the family in society – and social policy.

Under the directorship of the home secretary, Jack Straw, this green paper was aimed at strengthening both the family and marriage. Once again, 'family' here means two opposite-sex parents. The family was seen as vital to moral stability in society, whilst divorce and single parenthood were viewed as potentially disruptive and damaging both to children and to society as a whole.

In a speech in October 1993, Tony Blair, who was shadow home secretary at the time, argued that 'the response of the left should be to acknowledge the importance of the family but to set the family within the broader community, just as the individual exists within the family' (*The Guardian* 1998). Furthermore, the Labour home secretary, Jack Straw, commented that 'it plainly makes sense for the Government to do what it can to strengthen the institution of marriage' (*ibid.*).

After the Labour government swept to power in the UK in a massive landslide victory in 1997, it continued many of the family policies it has inherited from the Conservative New Right. As mentioned, many of their policy decisions were based on the notion of the 'Third Way' – a view that there should be a balancing of the role of the state to interfere with peoples' lives, and the obligations and responsibilities of individuals and families to be independent and 'stand on their own feet'. In other words, this was an attempt to steer a path between the high public spending associated with Old Labour and savage cuts associated with the New Right governments of Thatcher and Major.

In 1997, Labour accepted the need to recognize diversity in the forms the family was taking. Rather than vilifying lone parents, it provided financial support for child care to get mothers back to work. The rights of homosexuals were improved, in terms of adoption and civil partnerships. In the Green Paper *Supporting Families,* stable relationships in marriage and the importance of the traditional family to help to counter the effects of deprivation and child poverty were identified. Following from the paper, the Family and Parenting Institute was set up to provide early intervention in the lives of children and their parents through a variety of projects – such as the Parenting Fund, the School–Parent Partnership, the Early Learning Partnership and others, in an attempt to create environments to enable families to help themselves alongside the appropriate guidance and advice.

The the Family and Parenting Institute website declared 'there's no such thing as an average family' and introduced a project called 'Knowing families', which aimed through research to find out what families expected and wanted from family social policy, and thereby match changes to these expectations.

Through the late 1990s and into the early years of the 2000s, various significant policies were introduced. In 2003, 'Every Child Matters' was introduced in an attempt to draw together children's services and those who work with children to ensure their safety and protection. Following a number of high-profile deaths of children at the hands of their relatives, the government wanted to ensure no other child 'slipped through the net'. A Minister for Children was also appointed in that year – Margaret Hodge. In 2004, Sure Start Centres were set up across the country to provide for the health, well-being and early education of children, particularly those from deprived or poor backgrounds. Once again, the idea of early intervention was believed to be the right course of action in preventing the cycle of disadvantage.

After Gordon Brown succeeded Tony Blair as the UK's prime minister in 2007, much of the emphasis on strong families was maintained, but diversity in family structure still continued to be recognized. Brown continued the former family policies: a commitment to ending child poverty – giving benefits to, but attempting to improve employability of, lone parents through the New Deal and the setting up of child trust funds. The Conservative leader David Cameron, who became prime minister in 2010, in the Coalition government with the Liberal Democrats, seemed reluctant to alienate people by blaming the ills of society on single parents but, instead, emphasized the advantages to children and society of strong, stable, conventional two-parent households. An outline of their policy statements connected to the family has been given (pp. 209–10).

THE COALITION GOVERNMENT 2010

As the first Coalition government formed in the UK since World War II, it is unclear how the Conservatives and Liberal Democrats will work together on policies. The Coalition government resulted from the 2010 general election result, which failed to elect a government with an overall majority, and there is no blueprint for its operation and organization. Both parties have said they will compromise and try to ensure stable government. As you

Exercise 11.10

Lone parenthood seems to be a central issue for both the New Right and the New Left, and it has become an important policy issue. Why do you think this is so? Why do politicians consider it an important area of debate?

Look back to the views of the functionalists and feminists on this issue (Chapters 3 and 4).

1. How do each of these perspectives see the lone-parent family? Write a summary of each.
2. Do the theories give us any clues as to why the growth or decline of this type of family should be considered so important?

Exam focus

1. Outline and explain four social policies that reinforce the traditional model of the family. Describe and evaluate how each policy brings this about.
2. Critically assess the connections between socio-political perspectives and the development of social policies on the family during the period 1979–2010.

Important concepts

New Right • New Left • Communitarianism • Neo-functionalism • Thatcherism • Third Way • Civil partnerships • Coalition government

Critical thinking

1. How far do you agree with Giddens that the main political parties share similar social policies on the family?
2. Is it still the case that women, as wives and mothers, are at the centre of social policy development on the family? How should this change, given that many mothers now work?
3. The UK Coalition government of 2010 brought together the Conservative and Liberal Democratic parties in government. To what extent were the Coalition government's policies on the family a fusion of the parties' individual approaches to the family?

Bibliography

Abbott, P. and Wallace, C. (1992) *The Family and the New Right* (London: Pluto Press).
Abbott, P. and Wallace, C. (1997) *An Introduction to Sociology: Feminist Perspectives*, 2nd edn (London: Routledge).
Acker, J. (1989) 'The Problem with Patriarchy', *Sociology* 23(2).
Alcock, P. (1996) *Social Policy in Britain* (London: Macmillan).
Alexander, C., Duncan, S. and Edwards, R. (2010) *Teenage Parents. What's The Problem?* (London: Tufnell Press).
Alford-Cooper, F. (1998) *For Keeps: Marriages That Last A Lifetime* (Armonk, NY: Sharpe).
Allan, G. (2009) 'Family and Friends in Today's World', *Sociology Review* 19(1).
Allan, G. and Crow, G. (2001) *Families, Households and Society* (Basingstoke: Palgrave).
Althusser, L. (1971) *Lenin and Philosophy and Other Essays* (London: New Left Books).
Amato, P.R. (2001) 'Children of Divorce in the 1990s: An Update of the Amato and Keith (1991) Meta-Analysis', *Journal of Family Psychology* 15: 355–70.
Amos, V. and Parmar, P. (1984) 'Challenging Imperial Feminism', *Feminist Review* 17.
Anderson, M. (1971) *Family Structure in Nineteenth Century Lancashire* (Cambridge: Cambridge University Press).
Andersson, G. (1998) 'Trends in Marriage Formation in Sweden 1971–1993', *European Journal of Population* 14: 157–78.
Archard, D. (1993) *Children: Rights and Childhood* (London: Routledge).
Arendell, T. (2000) 'Conceiving and Investigating Motherhood: The Decade's Scholarship' *Journal of Marriage and Family* 62(4): 1192–1207.
Ariès, P. (1973) *Centuries of Childhood* (Harmondsworth: Penguin).
Ariès, P. (1981) *The Hour of Our Death* (London: Penguin).
Badgett, M.V.L. (2009) *When Gay People Get Married* (New York: New York University Press).
Ballard, R. (1982) 'South Asian Families', in R.N. Rapoport, Fogarty, M.P. and Rapoport, R. (eds), *Families in Britain* (London: Routledge & Kegan Paul).
Barlow, K. and Chapin, B.L. (2010) 'The Practicing of Mothering: An Introduction', *Ethos* 38(4): 324–38.
Barrett, M. and McIntosh, M. (1982) *The Anti-Social Family* (London: Verso).
Barrett, M. and McIntosh, M. (1991) *The Anti-Social Family*, 2nd edn (London: Verso).
Barrow, J. (1982) 'West Indian Families: An Insider's Perspective', in R.N. Rapoport, Fogarty, M.P. and Rapoport, R. (eds), *Families in Britain* (London: Routledge & Kegan Paul).
Bauman, Z. (1990) *Thinking Sociologically* (Oxford: Blackwell).
Bauman, Z. (2003) *Liquid Love: On the Frailty of Human Bonds* (Cambridge: Polity).
Beardsworth, A. and Keil, T. (1993) 'Hungry for Knowledge: The Sociology of Food and Eating', *Sociology Review* 3(2): 11–15.
Beauvoir, S. de (1953) *The Second Sex* (Harmondsworth: Penguin).
Beck, U. (1992) *Risk Society: Towards A New Modernity* (London: Sage).
Beck, U. and Beck-Gernsheim, E. (1995) *The Normal Chaos of Love* (Cambridge: Polity Press).
Beck, U. and Beck-Gernsheim, E. (2002) *Individualization* (London: Sage).
Beck, U., Giddens, A. and Lash, S. (1994) *Reflexive Modernization: Politics, Tradition and Aesthetics in the Modern Social Order* (Cambridge: Polity Press).

Elias, N. (1982) *The Civilizing Process, Vol. 2: State Formation and Civilisation* (Oxford: Basil Blackwell).
Elias, N. (1985) *The Loneliness of the Dying* (Oxford: Basil Blackwell).
Elias, N. (1992) *Time: An Essay* (Oxford: Basil Blackwell).
Elliot, F. (1986) *The Family: Change or Consistency* (London: Macmillan).
Elliot, F.R. (1996) *Gender, Family and Society* (Basingstoke: Macmillan).
Engels, F. (1972) *The Origin of the Family, Private Property and the State* (New York: Pathfinder Press).
ESRC (2003) 'Grandparenthood: Its Meaning and Its Contribution to Older People's Lives', *Growing Older Programme*, Research Findings 22.
Etzioni, A. (1995) *The Spirit of Community* (London: Fontana).
Eversley, D. and Bonnerjea, L. (1982) 'Social Change and Indicators of Diversity', in R.N. Rapoport, Fogarty, M.P. and Rapoport, R. (eds), *Families in Britain* (London: Routledge & Kegan Paul).
Fagotto, M., Borga, U L. and Musumeci, G. (2010) *On the Frontline against Africa's Bush Killers*. Available at http://www.guardian.co.uk/world/2010/may/16/dispatch-on-frontline-with-bush-killers [Last accessed 7 June 2010].
Farlax. (2011) *The Free Dictionary* Online: http://www.thefreedictionary.com/family [Last accessed 17 November 2011].
Featherstone, M. (1991) *Consumer Culture and Postmodernism* (London: Sage).
Featherstone, M. and Hepworth, M. (1991) 'The Mask of Aging and the Postmodern Life Course', in M. Featherstone, M. Hepworth and B.S. Turner (eds), *The Body: Social Process and Cultural Theory* (London: Sage).
Finch J. (2007) 'Displaying Families' *Sociology* 41(1).
Finch, J. (1989) *Family Obligations and Social Change* (Cambridge: Polity Press).
Finch, J. and Mason, J. (1993) *Negotiating Family Responsibilities* (London: Routledge).
Finkelhor, D. and Hotaling, G.T. (1984) 'Sexual Abuse in the National Incidence Study of Child Abuse and Neglect', *Child Abuse and Neglect* 8(1).
Firestone, S. (1979) *The Dialectic of Sex: The Case for Feminist Revolution* (London: Women's Press).
Fletcher, R. (1966) *The Family and Marriage in Britain* (Harmondsworth: Penguin).
Folgerø, T. (2008) 'Queer Nuclear Families? Reproducing or Transgressing Heteronormativity', *Journal of Homosexuality* 54(1).
Foucault, M. (1977) *Discipline and Punish: The Birth of the Prison* (Harmondsworth: Penguin).
Foucault, M. (1979) *The History of Sexuality: Volume One – An Introduction* (London: Penguin).
Foucault, M. (1984) *The Foucault Reader: An Introduction to Foucault's Thought* (ed. P. Rabinow) (London: Penguin).
Foucault, M. (1985) *The Use of Pleasure: The History of Sexuality*, Volume 2 (London: Penguin).
Foucault, M. (1986) *The Care of the Self: The History of Sexuality*, Volume 3 (London: Penguin).
Fuller-Thomson, E. and Minkler, M. (2001) 'American Grandparents Providing Extensive Child Care to Their Grandchildren', *Gerontologist* 41: 201–9.
Furstenberg, F. (1999) 'Children and Family Change: Discourse between Social Scientists and the Media', *Contemporary Sociology* 28: 10–17.
Garey, A.I. (1999) *Weaving Work and Motherhood* (Philadelphia: Temple University Press).
Gatrell, C. (2008) 'Involved Fatherhood', *Sociology Review* 18(1).
Gavron, H. (1966) *The Captive Wife: Conflicts of Housebound Mothers* (Harmondsworth: Penguin).
Giddens, A. (1984) *The Constitution of Society: Outline of the Theory of Structuration* (Cambridge: Polity Press).
Giddens, A. (1986) *Sociology: A Brief But Critical Introduction*, 2nd edn (London: Macmillan).
Giddens, A. (1989) *Sociology* (Cambridge: Polity Press).
Giddens, A. (1991a) *The Consequences of Modernity* (Cambridge: Polity Press).
Giddens, A. (1991b) *Modernity and Self-Identity: Self and Society in the Late Modern Age* (Cambridge: Polity Press).
Giddens, A. (1992) *The Transformation of Intimacy: Sexuality, Love and Eroticism in Modern Societies* (Cambridge: Polity Press).
Giddens, A. (1994) *Beyond Left and Right: The Future of Radical Politics* (Cambridge: Polity Press).

Giddens, A. (1996) *In Defence of Sociology: Essays, Interpretations and Rejoinders* (Cambridge: Polity Press).
Gillespie, R. (2001) 'Contextualising Voluntary Childlessness within a Postmodern Model of Reproduction: Implications for Health and Social Needs', *Critical Social Policy* 21: 139–59.
Gittins, D. (1993) *The Family in Question: Changing Households and Familiar Ideologies*, 2nd edn (Basingstoke: Macmillan).
Glaser, K., Tomassini, C. and Stuchbury, R. (2008) 'Differences Over Time in the Relationship between Partnership Disruptions and Support in Early Old Age in Britain', *Journal of Gerontology: Social Sciences* 63B S359–S368.
Glenn, E.N. (1994) 'Social Constructions of Mothering: A Thematic Overview', in E.N. Glenn, G. Chang, and L.R. Forcey (eds), *Mothering: Ideology, Experience and Agency* (New York: Routledge).
Goffman, E. (1969) *The Presentation of Self in Everyday Life* (Harmondsworth: Penguin).
Goldthorpe, J.H. (1987) *Social Mobility and Class Structure in Modern Britain* (Oxford: Clarendon Press).
Goldthorpe, J.H. Lockwood, D., Bechhofer, F. and Platt, J. (1969) *The Affluent Worker in the Class Structure* (Cambridge: Cambridge University Press).
Goode, W. (1963) *World Revolution and Family Patterns* (New York: Free Press).
Gough, K. (1959) 'Is the Family Universal? The Nayar Case', in N.W. Bell and E.F. Vogel (eds), *A Modern Introduction to the Family* (London: Collier-Macmillan).
Gramsci, A. (1971 [1929–35]) *Selections from the Prison Notebooks* (ed. Q. Hoare) (London: Lawrence & Wishart).
Gramsci, A. (1977) *Selections from Political Writings, 1910–1920* (ed. Q. Hoare) (London: Lawrence & Wishart).
Gramsci, A. (1978) *Selections from Political Writings, 1921–1926* (ed. Q. Hoare) (London: Lawrence & Wishart).
Guardian, The (1998) Article concerning the importance of the family, 3 November: 17.
Guardian, The (2010) Article by Chris McGreal in Washington, 19 January.
Hakim, C. (1995) 'Five Feminist Myths about Women's Employment', *British Journal of Sociology* 46(3).
Halsey, A.H. (1986) *Change in British Society*, 3rd edn (Oxford: Oxford University Press).
Hantrais, L., Filipov, D. and Billari, F. C. (2006) *Policy Implications of Changing Family Formation* (Strasbourg: Council of Europe).
Hao, L. and Xie, G. (2002) 'The Complexity and Endogeneity of Family Structure in Explaining Children's Behavior', *Social Science Research* 31: 1–28.
Haralambos, M. and Heald, R. (1985) *Sociology Themes and Perspectives* (London: University Tutorial Press).
Haraven, T.K. (1994) 'Recent Research on the History of the Family', in M. Drake (ed.), *Time, Family and Community* (Oxford: Blackwell).
Hartmann, H. (1979) 'The Unhappy Marriage of Marxism and Feminism: Towards A More Progressive Union', *Capital and Class* 3(2).
Harvey, D. (1989) *The Condition of Postmodernity* (Oxford: Blackwell).
Hatch, L.R. (2000) *Beyond Gender Differences* (Amityville, NY: Baywood).
Hauari, H. and Hollingworth, K. (2009) *Understanding Fathering: Masculinity, Diversity and Change* (York: Joseph Rowntree Foundation).
Hays, S. (1996) *The Cultural Contradictions of Motherhood* (New Haven, CT: Yale University Press).
Heidensohn, F. (1996) *Women and Crime*, 2nd edn (Basingstoke: Macmillan).
Henriques, F. and Slaughter, C. (1956) *Coal is our Life* (London: Eyre & Spottiswoode).
Hetherington, E.M. and Kelly, J. (2002) *For Better or Worse* (New York: Norton).
Hill, Amelia (2010) 'In Focus', *The Observer*, 21 February 2010: 16.
Hockey, J. and James, A. (1993) *Growing Up and Growing Old: Ageing and Dependency in the Life Course* (London: Sage).
Hrdy, S.B. (2009) *Mothers and Others: The Evolutionary Origins of Mutual Understanding* (Cambridge, MA: Harvard University Press).

Pleck, J.H. and Masciadrelli, B.P. (2003) 'Parental Involvement: Levels, Sources and Consequences', in M.E. Lamb (ed.), *The Role of the Father in Child Development*, 4th edn (New York: John Wiley).

Plummer, K. (1995) *Telling Sexual Stories, Power, Change and Social* Worlds (London: Routledge).

Popenoe, D. (1996) 'Modern Marriage: Revising the Cultural Script', in D. Popenhoe, J. Elshtain and D. Blankenhorn (eds) *Promises to Keep* (Lanham, MD: Rowman & Littlefield).

Postman, N. (1985) *The Disappearance of Childhood: How TV is Changing Children's Lives* (London: W. H. Allen).

Poulantzas, N. (1980) *State Power Socialism* (London: New Left Books).

Raley, R.K. (2000) 'Recent Trends and Differentials in Marriage and Cohabitation', in L.J. White, C. Bachrach, M. Hindin, E. Thompson and A. Thornton (eds), *The Ties that Bind* (New York: Aldine de Gruyter).

Rapoport, R. (1989) 'Ideologies about Family Forms – Towards Diversity', in K. Boh, M. Bak and C. Clason (eds), *Changing Patterns of European Family Life* (London: Routledge).

Rapoport, R.N., Fogarty, M.P. and Rapoport, R. (eds) (1982) *Families in Britain* (London: Routledge & Kegan Paul).

Rees, A. (1950) *Life in a Welsh Countryside* (Cardiff: University of Wales).

Renvoize, J. (1985) *Going Solo: Single Mothers by Choice* (London: Routledge & Kegan Paul).

Reynolds, T. (2008) *Ties that Bind: Families, Social Capital and Caribbean Second-generation Return Migration* (London: South Bank University and University of Sussex).

Ridge, T. (2008) 'Research on Children in Families' *Sociology Review* 18(1).

Roopnarine, J.L. and U.P. Gielen (2005) *Families in Global Perspective* (London: Pearson).

Roseneil, S. (2000) 'Queer Frameworks and Queer Tendencies: Towards an Understanding of Postmodern Transformations of Sexuality', *Sociological Research Online*, 5(3).

Roseneil, S. and Budgeon, S. (2004) 'Cultures of Intimacy and Care beyond 'the Family': Personal Life and Social Change in the Early 21st Century', *Current Sociology* 52(2).

Rosser, R. and C. Harris (1965) *The Family and Social Change* (London: Routledge & Kegan Paul).

Rowlingson, K. and McKay, S. (1998) *The Growth of Lone Parenthood* (London: Policy Study Institute).

Salway, S. and Chowbray, P. (2009) *Understanding the Experiences of Asian Fathers in Britain* (York: Joseph Rowntree Foundation).

Sanchez-Taylor, J. (2010) 'Sex Tourism – Crime, Romance or Exploitation?', *Sociology Review* 19(4).

Sapsford, R. (1995) 'Endnote: Public and Private', in J. Muncie, M. Wetherell, M. Langan, R. Dallos and A. Douglas Cochrane (eds), *Understanding the Family* (London: Sage).

Sargent, L. (ed.) (1981) *The Unhappy Marriage of Marxism and Feminism: A Debate on Class and Patriarchy* (London: Pluto Press).

Sassetti, M. R. (1993) 'Domestic Violence', in B.A. Elliott, K.C. Halverson and M.K. Hendricks-Matthews (eds), *Primary Care: Family Violence and Abusive Relationships* (Philadelphia, PA: W.B. Saunders).

Scanzoni, J. (1993) 'New Action Theory and Contemporary Families', *Journal of Family Issues* 14(1).

Scanzoni, J. (2004) 'Household Diversity: The Starting Point for Healthy Families in the New Century', in M. Coleman and L.H. Ganong, *Handbook of Contemporary Families* (Thousand Oaks: Sage).

Scott, J. and Braun, M. (2006) 'Individualization of Family Values?' in P. Ester, M. Braun and P. Mohler (eds) *Globalization, Value Change and Generations* (Leiden: Brill).

Scott J., Treas, J. and Richards, M. (2004) *The Blackwell Companion to the Sociology of Families* (Oxford: Blackwell Publishing).

Scruton, R. (1990) *The Philosopher on Dover Beach* (Manchester: Carcanet).

Segal, L. (1987) *Is the Future Female*? (London: Virago).

Seltzer, J. A. (2004) 'Cohabitation and Family Change', in M. Coleman and L.H. Ganong, *Handbook of Contemporary Families* (Thousand Oaks: Sage).

Shilling, C. (1993) *The Body and Social Theory* (London: Sage).

Shorter, E. (1975) *The Making of the Modern Family* (London: Fontana).

Silverstein, L.B. and Auerbach, C.F. (2005) '(Post)modern families', in J.L. Roopnarine and U.P. Gielen (2005), *Families in Global Perspective* (London: Pearson).

Smart, C. and Shipman, B. (2004) 'Visions in Monochrome: Families, Marriage and the Individualization Thesis', *British Journal of Sociology* 55(4).
Smith, J. (1997) *Different for Girls: How Culture Creates Women* (London: Chatto & Windus).
Social Exclusion Unit (1999) *Teenage Pregnancy* (London, HMSO Cm 4342).
Somerville, J. (2000) *Feminism and the Family: Politics and Society in the UK and USA* (Basingstoke: Macmillan).
Speier, M. (1976) 'The Child as Conversationalist: Some Culture Contact Features of Conversational Interactions between Adults and Children', in M. Hammersley and P. Woods (eds), *The Process of Schooling: A Sociological Reader* (London: Routledge & Kegan Paul).
Spencer, H. (1971) *Structure, Function and Evolution* (London: Nelson).
Stacey, J. (1990) *Brave New Families* (New York: Basic Books).
Stacey J. (2002) 'Fellow Families? Genres of Gay Male Intimacy and Kinship in a Global Metropolis', CAVA International Seminar Paper Online: www.leeds.ac.uk/cava/papers/intseminar3stacey.htm.
Stacey, J. (1997) *In the Name of the Family; Rethinking Family Values in the Postmodern Age* (Boston: Beacon Press).
Stanley, L. (1992) 'Changing Households? Changing Work?', in N. Abercrombie and A. Warde (eds), *Social Change in Contemporary Britain* (Cambridge: Polity Press).
Starkey, D. (1995) 'The Family in History', Lecture presented to Updates Conference, Manchester.
Stone, L. (1977) *The Family, Sex and Marriage in England 1500–1800* (London: Weidenfeld & Nicolson).
Sunar, D. and G. Fizşek (2005) 'Contemporary Turkish Families', in J.L.Roopnarine and U.P. Gielen *Families in Global Perspective* (London: Pearson).
Taylor, S. (1988) 'Researching Child Abuse' in R. Burgess (ed.) *Investigating Society* (London: Longman).
Taylor, S. (1992) 'Measuring Child Abuse', *Sociology Review* 1(3).
Tedston, A. (2009) *Hospital Choices* Available at http://209.85.229.132/search?q=cache:LCKNWoIVPgYJ:www.hospitalchoices.co.uk/NewsDetails.aspx%3FArticleId%3D3539+Dr+Alison+Tedston+2009/10&cd=1&hl=en&ct=clnk&gl=uk [Last accessed 7 June 2010].
Thompson, K. (1998) *Moral Panics* (London: Routledge).
Thorne, B. (1982) *Feminist Rethinking of the Family: An Overview* (New York: Longman).
Tiger, L. and Fox, R. (1972) *The Imperial Animal* (London: Seccker & Warburg).
Toffler, A. (1971) *Future Shock* (London: Pan).
Trowler, P. (1989) *Investigating Health, Welfare and Poverty* (London: Unwin Hyman).
Tucker, M.B. (2000) 'Considerations in the Development of Family Policy for African Americans', in J.S. Jackson (ed.) *New Directions: African Americans in a Diversifying Nation* (Washington: National Policy Association).
Tunstall, J. (1962) *The Fishermen* (London: MacGibbon & Kee).
Turner, B.S. (1984) *The Body and Society: Explorations in Social Theory* (Oxford: Blackwell).
Valentine, G., Skelton, T. and Butler, R. (2003) 'Coming Out and Outcomes: Negotiating Lesbian and Gay Identities with, and in, the Family', *Environment and Planning D; Society and Space* 21(4).
Viner, K. (2005) 'A Year of Killing', *The Guardian*. 10 December. Available at http://www.guardian.co.uk/uk/2005/dec/10/ukcrime.prisonsandprobation [Last accessed 7 June 2010].
Walby, S. (1986) *Patriarchy at Work* (Cambridge: Polity Press).
Walby, S. (1988) 'Gender, Politics and Social Theory', *Sociology* 22(2).
Walby, S. (1990) *Theorising Patriarchy* (Oxford: Blackwell).
Wallerstein, J. and Blakeslee, S. (1989) *Second Choices* (London: Bantam).
Walter, N. (1999) *The New Feminism* (London: Little, Brown).
Walter, N. (2010) *Living Dolls: The Return of Sexism* (London: Virago).
Walzer, S. (2009) 'Redoing Gender through Divorce', *Journal of Social and Personal Relationships* 25(1).
Weber, M. (1930) *The Protestant Ethic and the Spirit of Capitalism* (London: Allen & Unwin; first published 1905).
Weeks, J., Heaphy, B. and Donovan, C. (2001) *Same-Sex Intimacies: Families of Choice and Other Life Experiments* (London: Routledge).